The Xinjiang Conflict:
Uyghur Identity, Language Policy, and Political Discourse

Policy Studies 15

The Xinjiang Conflict:
Uyghur Identity, Language Policy, and Political Discourse

Arienne M. Dwyer

The Xinjiang Conflict: Uyghur Identity, Language Policy, and Political Discourse
by Arienne M. Dwyer

ISBN   1-932728-28-7 (print version)
ISSN   1547-1349 (print version)

Online at: www.eastwestcenterwashington.org/publications

East-West Center Washington
1819 L Street, NW, Suite 200
Washington, D.C.   20036

Tel: (202) 293-3995
Fax: (202) 293-1402

E-mail: publications@eastwestcenterwashington.org

Website: www.eastwestcenterwashington.org

The *Policy Studies* series contributes to the Center's role as a forum for discussion of key contemporary domestic and international political, economic, and strategic issues affecting Asia. The views expressed are those of the author(s) and not necessarily those of the Center.

This publication is a product of the East-West Center Washington project on *Managing Internal Conflicts in Asia*. For details, see pages 95–103.

The project and this publication are supported by a generous grant from the Carnegie Corporation of New York.

Contents

List of Acronyms

CCTV	Chinese Central Television
CCP	Chinese Communist Party
ETIM	Eastern Turkestan Islamic Movement
FTO	Foreign Terrorist Organization
HSK	the first standardized test for assessing the Chinese competence of non-native speakers
PRC	People's Republic of China
UNESCO	United Nations Educational, Scientific, and Cultural Organization
XUAR	Xinjiang Uyghur Autonomous Region

Executive Summary

This study explores Chinese language policy and language use in Inner Asia, as well as the relation of language policy to the politics of Uyghur identity. Language is central to ethnic identity, and official language policies are often overlooked as critical factors in conflict over ethnic nationalism. In Chinese Inner Asia, any solution to ethnic conflict will include real linguistic and cultural autonomy for major ethnic groups.

Language policy has been at the heart of Chinese nation building. Shortly after the inception of the People's Republic of China (PRC), language policy in China's border regions was responsive to local conditions and arguably one of the more flexible in the world. In the last 15 years, however, although China's official language policy has remained constant, its covert language policy has become increasingly reactive, and tied to geopolitical considerations. This trend has been particularly salient in the Xinjiang Uyghur Autonomous Region (XUAR), where multilingualism and cultural pluralism have been progressively curtailed in favor of a monolingual, monocultural model, and a concomitant rise of an oppositional modern Uyghur identity. This study traces the evolution of the PRC government's minorities-language policy by evaluating two principal actors (the PRC and the Uyghurs) as well as two peripheral collective actors (first, the newly independent Central Asian republics, and second, North America and Europe). The peripheral groups are relevant to how the PRC has implemented and refined its language policy in border regions. Recent policy shifts in neighboring Central Asian republics (with their Turkic-speaking populations) serve as valuable comparisons with how China has handled its minority-language cases. In contrast, North America and Europe were not relevant for Chinese minority policy until September 2001. But since 9/11, skillful Chinese government media rhetoric has drawn these countries—especially the United States—unwittingly into China's domestic minority-nationalism issues.

The PRC's original language policy in its border regions, which was integrationist but not assimilative, was well founded and generally well received by both party officials and by the national minorities themselves. Such a pluralistic policy, which arguably supported both national stability and local ethnic groups, stood out positively in comparison with Soviet policies of the time. Yet beginning in the mid-1980s, Beijing began to shift from cultural accommodation towards an overt policy of assimilation. This shift only served to reinforce both Uyghur nationalism and small separatist movements, with potential to undermine the territorial integrity of the PRC and the Chinese effort to build a modern Chinese nation. This policy shift has been counterproductive. Supporting the maintenance of Uyghur language and identity is not antithetical to the Chinese goal of nation building. In fact, it would ultimately support that goal.

In addition to the PRC's overt language policy, including language education and standardization, its covert policy of minority acculturation and assimilation has become more prominent, as reflected in its recent use of discourse characterizing Uyghur nationalist movements as terrorist. The United States, through its so-called "war on terror[ism]," allowed itself to be misled by post-9/11 Chinese media reports on the relationship between the Uyghurs and Islamic militants. In so doing, the United States has conflated Uyghur nationalism with "terrorism," thus justifying U.S.-Chinese government collaboration in the Chinese Communist Party's project to suppress its own minorities. Chinese media rhetoric describing Uyghur nationalists before and after 2001 shows a clearly demarcated shift from "separatists" to "Islamic terrorists" as it named over fifty Uyghur "terrorist groups." Most Western media, which previously had paid little attention to western China, have followed suit, equating these fringe separatist groups with terrorists. Unfortunately, all eight to 10 million Uyghurs have become guilty by association: Washington's recognition of just one of these separatist groups as officially terrorist has created a climate of mistrust in government and the public against the Uyghurs as a whole.

Both Beijing and Washington are about to lose crucial political opportunities in this far-flung territory. Beijing's new hard-line stance, which restricts even language and culture, has galled the many moderate Xinjiang citizens who once grudgingly accepted Chinese political restrictions as a price of regional economic development. The PRC government still has an opportunity to win back these people with a more pluralistic cultural policy that emphasizes support for Uyghur and other policy-relevant minority languages and that eases other cultural restrictions, particularly on religion. Without such a policy shift, as Beijing well knows, Xinjiang could become China's Kashmir. Yet if current PRC policy stays on course, any change is likely to be even more restrictive, since the government considers its cultural accommodation of the 1980s and 1990s to be a cause of unrest, rather than a solution to it.

The United States, for its part, must make clear to Beijing that current U.S. political imperatives will not distract U.S. policy from supporting human rights, including cultural rights. The Uyghurs have been among the most pro-American citizens in China. They also happen to be Muslims. If the United States wants international partners in fighting terrorism, it should cultivate a cooperative partnership with China, including the Uyghurs. If the Xinjiang region is to be involved in an initiative against international terrorism, then the United States can urge China and its allies to cultivate the Uyghurs—with their knowledge of the language and cultures of Central Asia—as partners rather than as opponents.

As Washington has begun to realize, its anti-Uyghur policies, even those targeted only at violent fringe groups, have already generated negative sentiment in Xinjiang towards the United States. Policies perceived as anti-Uyghur or anti-Muslim could well radicalize previously apolitical Uyghurs, pushing them into militant or radical Islamic groups.

This negotiation between state policies and ethnoreligious identity occurs within the matrix of language. While the PRC's official policy remains pluralistic, its unofficial policy has become increasingly assimilative. Such an apparent paradox is readily interpretable if we understand it as the simultaneous implementation of overt and covert policy. In a shift in media discourse from *Uyghur separatists* to *Muslim terrorists*, a covert language policy is being applied for international political ends. This manipulation of discourse about the Uyghurs is directly related to China's overall cultural policy towards its minorities. This study evaluates the theory and implementation of PRC language policy in Inner Asia. Uyghur is situated within a hierarchy of languages within Xinjiang, where it has become a supra-regional language but is clearly subordinate to the national Chinese language. Modernizing a language requires government and societal support for maintaining and diversifying the domains in which a language is used. I examine successes and failures of language policy implementation. Education is closely tied to both overt and covert language policy, and language education policy in Xinjiang reflects the assimilationist trend. Scholastic publishing, school choice, languages of instruction, and language instruction all entail sociopolitical policy decisions that have largely been made in view of economic and political stability, with Chinese materials and instruction rapidly gaining the upper hand. I examine issues in the instruction and use of Uyghur and other native languages, Standard Chinese, and English. Uyghur nationalists, whose reinvigorated sentiment is an unintended result of China's minorities policy, have been distrustful of and dismayed at China's apparent intentions for development of the region, which appears to bring yet more monoculturalism in the form of Han favoritism and cultural assimilation. The Uyghur response to language policy thus bears directly on China's overarching concern of regional stability. I propose policy adjustments that China and the United States might consider to mitigate these effects.

The Xinjiang Conflict:
Uyghur Identity, Language Policy, and Political Discourse

The Western Hu are far away.
They live in an outer zone.

Their countries' products are beautiful and precious,
But their character is debauched and frivolous.

They do not follow the rites of China.
Han has the canonical books.

They do not obey the Way of the Gods.
How pitiful!
How obstinate!

– Epilogue to the *History of the Later Han dynasty (Hou Han Shu)*[1]

Early Chinese historians wrote how the ways of the "Western Hu," or early Central and Inner Asians, in no way conformed to Chinese norms. In recent times, relations with the Uyghurs, who are some of the distant descendants of the Hu, have provoked a similar frustration in the PRC.

In response to what the PRC considers its failed 1980s policy of cultural liberalization in Xinjiang, China has in recent years moved rapidly to implement a new policy of Chinese monoculturalism in the region. Though Chinese population transfers to Xinjiang and economic disparities have also exacerbated tensions between Chinese and Uyghurs, it is minority-language policy which has brought the mutual discontent of Uyghurs and the central Chinese government to a head. Many ordinary Uyghurs have interpreted recent language policies—which include the expansion of Chinese language domains in education and the media as well as a reduction of minority-language domains—as a direct assault on Uyghur culture. Yet Beijing sees these policy changes as necessary to ensure political stability for the continued economic development of the region.

The roots of the Xinjiang conflict can only be understood by examining official *and* unofficial policy. The PRC's official (overt) cultural policy is egalitarian and accommodationist. But its unofficial (covert) policy has since the 1980s focused on assimilating Xinjiang's major minorities, particularly the Uyghurs, to the dominant Chinese culture. This study traces both the theory and implementation of official language policies in China's border regions from the founding of the PRC to the present day. It also examines the concurrent systematic implementation of covert policies, particularly in the domains of education and the media. Since 2001, accounts of the Xinjiang conflict have appeared with increasing frequency in the international press. While many Western media services have implied that the source of conflict in Xinjiang lies in cultural differences between Uyghurs and Chinese, the Chinese press has recently ascribed almost all dissent to international terrorism. The latter rhetoric is part of the larger monoculturalist Chinese language policy, which carefully manages the connotations of terms such as "Eastern Turkestan," "Muslim," and "terrorist." This study argues that United States policy towards separatism in Xinjiang has been significantly influenced by this managed discourse of the Chinese press.

Monoculturalist policies have contributed to a destabilization of the region. China has an opportunity to reverse this trend by implementing an updated version of its official multiculturalist language policy. A number of specific policy recommendations for China and the United States are given at the end of this work.

Xinjiang, the Uyghurs, and the Xinjiang Conflict

The territory in which the Uyghurs live is of enormous political, economic, and demographic significance for the Beijing government. Known officially as the Xinjiang Uyghur Autonomous Region (XUAR), Xinjiang constitutes about one-sixth of China's landmass, borders on eight Central Asian countries, provides a number of critical natural resources sustaining China's economic growth, and is a major population safety valve for resettling Han Chinese from central China. The area—a diamond-shaped territory of two basins ringed and bisected by mountains—is also home to a number of non-Hans, primarily Turkic peoples. Besides a Uyghur population of officially 8.2 million (as of the 2002 census), Xinjiang is also home to smaller populations of Kazakhs, Kyrgyz, Oyrat Mongols, Sibes (related to Manchus), Chinese Muslims (Huis), and other groups.

The previously obscure titular ethnic group of the XUAR, the Uyghurs, has since 2001 attracted the attention of Western media for alleged involvement in "Islamic terrorism." Suddenly, Xinjiang and its peoples have become a topic of geopolitical significance for the United States. For China, Xinjiang is now the country's most politically sensitive.

For China, Xinjiang is now the country's most politically sensitive

At first glance, it appears China might have good reason to be concerned: mosque attendance is up, and formerly unknown radical-fundamentalist forms of Islam (and violence done in the name of Islam) are making limited inroads into the region. Yet this study argues that imported and/or militant Islam is unlikely to take hold as long as the Chinese government allows its major minorities sufficient cultural autonomy, including peaceful local forms of religious expression.

Most Uyghurs espouse a tempered, syncretic Sufism. While virtually all Uyghurs identify themselves as Muslims, what being Muslim entails varies considerably depending on locale and education. Islam appears to permeate most aspects of daily life in rural areas, while many urban Uyghurs only abstain from pork and observe a few major holidays. However, this urban/rural distinction is superficial; while urban Uyghurs may not pray five times a day at the mosque like their rural counterparts, Islam is nonetheless embedded in many of their daily activities, such as greetings and exclamations, mode of dress, scrupulous personal cleanliness (including the consumption of *halal* food), and a sense of solidarity with other Muslims in the world. For both urban and rural Uyghurs, ethnic identity is linked with religious and linguistic identity.

Western and Chinese media reports have alluded to "foreign" or "Arab" religious influence in Xinjiang. But imported forms of Salafi Islam have been and will continue to be largely unwelcome in Uyghur society. Youths will only become radicalized if they sense that their language and religion is under threat. If Beijing would support peaceful local forms of religious expression and the maintenance of major minority languages as it did in the 1980s, then the PRC will win back the support of many Uyghurs. This study argues that greater cultural autonomy, coupled with genuine economic opportunity, should be the focus of PRC policy in Xinjiang.

From establishing control over the region in the 1950s to the present day, the Chinese Communist Party (CCP) has made large investments in Xinjiang's economic development. The first priority of development has been the exploitation of raw materials. Xinjiang is believed to contain one-third of China's oil reserves (AP-Dow Jones July 2, 1996) as well as most of China's uranium, significant coal deposits, and many other minerals. Central Xinjiang, in a formerly Uyghur area about 265 kilometers southeast of Ürümchi, is a missile testing site, and was also the site of 44 nuclear tests (22 of them atmospheric) between 1964 and 1996.[2]

Most noticeable for local residents was the enormous influx of Han Chinese into Xinjiang, whose population increased from nearly 300,000 in 1953 to nearly 6 million in 1990, in addition to more than one-half million demobilized soldiers in the Production and Construction Corps. This influx created competition for Xinjiang's land and ecological resources. As of the 2000 census, Han Chinese made up 41 percent of Xinjiang's total population; their presence also exerts a strong dominant-language pressure on minority languages and cultures. Chinese encroachment on the region's natural and cultural resources has made activists and nationalists out of formerly apolitical minority people.

Chinese development of Xinjiang has included significant transportation and administrative infrastructure building. The rapid construction of roads, railroads, and cities facilitated the flow of goods and services from Inner China, the Central Asian republics, and Pakistan beginning in the 1980s. Xinjiang residents who traveled to these countries noticed that at least northern Xinjiang seemed better off than its neighbors: many more foodstuffs and goods were available in the markets. From these observations, some local people, particularly merchants and intellectuals, concluded that Chinese rule in Xinjiang, while not ideal, was a legitimate means of achieving economic development.

But the Chinese government began to lose this hard-won if tepid acceptance of its rule with the implementation of its hard-line campaign in Xinjiang beginning in 1996. As described below, the tumult and austerity of the Cultural Revolution in the 1960s was followed by a period of cultural and political liberalization in the 1980s. By the mid-1990s, however, the central Chinese government attributed isolated incidents of unrest to excessively lax cultural policies, and began a period of political and cultural crackdown that has lasted through the present. This overt political crackdown was accompanied by largely covert shifts in language and cultural policy aimed at further sinicizing the region.

I thus evaluate the Xinjiang conflict through the prism of language, exploring three distinct themes: overt language policy and its implementation, Uyghur nationalism, and covert language policy and political discourse.

Geographic Scope

As a contiguous area, Chinese Inner Asia boasts the largest concentration of fluent non-Chinese speakers within China.[3] Of these peoples, those with significant populations and territories—the Uyghurs, Tibetans, and Mongols—each have standardized prestige language forms (*acrolects*) as well as a large body of written literary and historical material. In addition to the flagship standard languages of these three groups, a plethora of dialects and non-standard language varieties also exist. Under these complex multilingual circumstances, language policy—be it covert or overt—is an integral part of virtually any policy decision for these regions.

We focus here on China's current western dominions in an ethnolinguistic and administrative sense. *Inner Asia* is the term that most closely describes the ethno-geographic region of this paper; however, the ethnic boundaries of Inner Asia extend beyond China's borders into Mongolia, south Siberia, and Central Asia. In China, Chinese Inner Asia is increasingly called simply *Xibu* ("the West"), particularly in reference to a large-scale group of government infrastructure projects aimed at developing poorer provinces and regions. Another term, *Xiyu* ("Western Regions") has been employed well over 2,000 years in both senses: historically, it referred both to territories under Chinese control west of inner China, and also to territories to the west of China. The term *Xiyu* in the sense of "Chinese Inner Asia" is widely used in China today, particularly in academic writing and television broadcasting. Its connotational vagueness and association with ancient empires serves well a political as well as geographic signifier.[4]

National-Level Language Planning for the Minorities of China

The Scope of Language Policy

Language planning, often overlooked as the arcane dominion of orthographic rules and bilingual signs, is actually one of the most effective tools for enacting social and public policy. Though language policy rarely makes headlines, it is a central tool in national consolidation and permeates all aspects of society. Language policy affects the domains, status, and use of language varieties and the rights of their speakers. It shapes the media, the education system, and provides a rallying point for or against ethnic identity; it is in turn shaped by economic, social, and geopolitical considerations.

Language planning entails two major aspects: internal and external. The internal aspects include the development and implementation of writing systems (graphization); the development of a normative language (standardization); modernization; and renovation. But since languages never exist in isolation, any examination of language planning must also include external aspects, including public and institutional discourse on building national and state identities of individual ethnic groups. In a highly multiethnic nation-state like China, language planning necessarily involves policy for both dominant as well as non-dominant groups; in a border area like Inner Asia, transnational discourses cannot be ignored.

Language planning…
is…one of the most
effective tools for
enacting social and
public policy

Every country has language policies, be they overt, covert, or both.[5] Overt policies are disseminated through legal documents, legislation, and official administrative bodies. Covert policies, which may promote or undermine languages, are unwritten and often not even discussed. They reflect policymakers' assumptions about the nature and comparative worth of ethnolinguistic groups and their speakers, and mesh so seamlessly with elite and popular ideologies that their existence is presumed a given. Being customary and "traditional," covert policies are implicit and must be inferred from praxis: from the implementation of overt policies, from media statements, and from popular language attitudes. Covert policies differ from mere opinions or attitudes in that they are systematically implemented in one or more domains (e.g., education and the media) over a period of time. The United States is an example of a nation without an overt policy specifically for language;[6] China has both overt and covert policies.

Raising Minority "Quality": Early Language Planning, 1949–79

Admirably, the founders of the People's Republic of China attended very early on to the establishment of official language policies that were both tolerant and promoted the languages of China. Nationwide, tolerance of linguistic diversity was enshrined in the Interim Constitution, allowing all recognized languages to continue to be used, though no resources were specified for their use. Designated minority areas on China's periphery (so-called Autonomous Regions, Prefectures, and Counties) enjoy written policies promoting minority languages. All languages, regardless of size and status, have legal guarantees; however, major minority languages in these Autonomous Regions are required to share space and resources with Standard Chinese in the domains of government administration, the courts, education, and the media.

The PRC was founded on the heady principles of equality for and unity of all officially recognized ethnic groups known as *minzu* ("nationalities").[7] Article 53 of the September 1949 Common Program (Interim Constitution), besides promoting a degree of local autonomy in areas with concentrations of minorities, stated simply that national minorities should have "*freedom to develop their dialects and languages, and to preserve or reform their traditions, customs, and religious beliefs*" (*Zhonghua...falü huibian* 1985, emphasis added).

Early PRC language policy was part of a broader economic and social development plan, which aimed to establish a new system of governance and society (eliminating imperialism and feudalism while establishing Marxism and egalitarianism) while also, crucially, building national unity. Based on Article 53, the stated goals of this period included support for officially recognized nationalities to use their own languages and writing systems. National minority education was to be promoted as a way to raise minority *suzhi* ("quality") (e.g., Liu and He 1989) as well as to train national minority cadres to fill posts in the local and Autonomous Region governments.

The perceived need to raise minority "quality" points to a fundamental contradiction between rational and emotional elements of China's minorities policy, a contradiction that has yet to be resolved 50 years after the founding of the PRC. The egalitarian aims of early Chinese communists contrasted sharply with the nearly universal perception on the part of Han Chinese elites that peripheral peoples (who, importantly, also included non-prestige Hans) were "backward" and "without culture."[8] This contradiction between rational egalitarianism and visceral anti-minority sentiment served and still serves to undermine proactive language-maintenance policies in China's Western Regions. Raising minority "quality" may be a laudable (if chauvinistic) sociological goal, yet at the same time, the connotations of *suzhi* were deeply insulting: In popular parlance across China, to be without *suzhi* is to be someone who spits and clips his nails in public.

In the early years of the People's Republic, national minority identification was seen as a key to nation building.[9] Each national minority had the constitutionally enshrined right to develop its own language and culture. Yet during the disastrous Great Leap Forward and Cultural Revolution of the late 1950s through the early 1970s, the linguistic egalitarianism of the Constitution was jettisoned in the name of Marxist revolution. The newly standardized form of northern Chinese known as *putonghua* ("the Common Language") became the flagship language associated with the new China; minority languages and cultural practices were to be shunned, as they were associated with "feudalism" or worse. It would be nearly 30 years before national minority-language planning again became a topic of public policy.[10]

The elite's disdain for non-prestige languages and cultures is not entirely due to political developments of the 20th century. Indeed, condescension towards ethnolinguistic groups on China's margins is a centuries-old custom that has developed into modern policy. Developments in 20th-century China have merely served to drape the reflexive dehumanization of minorities in new garb: Once termed "raw barbarians," now unassimilated minorities are sexy and in touch with nature and spirituality, while concomitantly of "low quality" and in need of Chinese civilization. Even in the late 20th century,

> *condescension...is a centuries-old custom that has developed into modern policy*

> [w]e...find [a] set of maps in the minds of Han [Chinese]: (1) the *barbarian minorities* of stagnation and backwardness; (2) the *sinicized minorities* as late-comers of development that have to catch up with the Han as quick as possible and to bring their economies and societies into line with that of the Han, and (c) the *delightful minorities* of prodigy, exotism, and esotericism (Heberer 2000:10).[11]

The Uyghurs fit all three of these profiles: The abject poverty of southern Xinjiang, together with unfavorable agricultural policies, has resulted in the economic stagnation of much of the region's population; the population of the better-off northern areas are more sinicized, yet are still playing linguistic and economic catch-up; and the oases of the entire Xinjiang region offer tourists the grace of Uyghur dance, the exotism of its Middle-Eastern sounding music,[12] and the safe esotericism of Sufi mysticism. These attitudes also pervade a collusive covert language policy that is part of a larger "civilizing project" (Harrell 1995) serving the ultimate goal of maintaining a unified Chinese state.

The early years of minority-language planning in the PRC were critical in establishing and legitimizing the "low quality" of national minority cultures and, by implication, peoples. Many policymakers genuinely believed that a policy of cultural improvement coupled with economic development was beneficial to minorities, whom they regarded as their "younger" brethren. Such attitudes were by no means limited to the Han Chinese; minority elites were also quick to judge less powerful groups as inferior. This situation was particularly true in Xinjiang, where centuries of oasis insularity has lead to a distrust of outsiders; this distrust even today can override the unifying modern identities of being Uyghur and Muslim.[13]

Public discourse strategies often served to subtly degrade minority "quality," even despite government efforts to the contrary. During the early years of the PRC, government scientists did make significant efforts to replace derogatory terms for non-Han peoples with more neutral ones: *Lolo* (now *Yi*); *Xifan* (now *Zang*—i.e., Tibetans and others); and *Man* ("southern barbarian"), whose Chinese character features an insect. Nowadays, pejorative ethnonyms have all but disappeared. One hopes that the few remaining exceptions (e.g., *Tu* ("local; hick") for Monguors, and *Gaoshan* ("high mountain") for nine Austronesian groups on Taiwan)[14] will also be replaced by neutral ethnonyms without the connotation of "lacking civilization, low quality."

Still, political expediency—demonstrating good will—was likely the key motivation for ethnonym replacement. Pejorative ethnonyms are still employed today for the forbearers of many minorities of China, with the tacit support of some Western scholars. For example, *Hu*, an ancient term for "barbarian" (i.e., northern and western non-Hans), continues to be used in modern historical works in and outside of China. In these works, references to the "Northern Barbarians" and "Western Hu" abound— including in art exhibition catalogues such as the unfortunately named *Traders and Raiders* exhibition (So & Bunker 1995).

Early minority-language policy, as part of minorities policy in general, was primarily pragmatic, yet influenced both by the overt egalitarian ideals of the Interim Constitution and a covert devaluation of minority languages. Establishing and fostering national unity required promoting Standard Mandarin Chinese to a dominant position at the expense of all other languages, including other varieties of Chinese. Promoting Standard Chinese entailed massive media and education campaigns to increase citizens' exposure to the language. In minority areas, the argument that minority languages were inherently low quality aided efforts to promote Standard Chinese: Minority languages were allegedly inadequate for the rigorous communicative demands of modern life, especially modern science.

As communicative domains for Standard Chinese expanded, those for minority languages shrank, reinforcing the notion that these languages were unimportant.[15] Ironically, if Inner Asian languages are indeed inferior, then northern Chinese (including Standard Chinese) must also be of low quality, since northern Chinese was radically changed by Altaic structures, i.e., from the ancestors of several of China's minorities in the Northwest (see for example Hashimoto 1984; Hashimoto 1986; and Wadley 1996).

From a comparative perspective, a given group need not be dominant to make the argument that its language is of superior quality to its neighbors, as the Chinese case seems to imply. In the postcolonial debate over India's national and regional standard languages, for example, the argumentation advanced was precisely opposite to that of the Chinese elite: In India, elites representing strong regional minority languages such as Tamil argued successfully that their languages were of *higher* quality than Hindi, and for this reason should be supported.[16]

Chinese minorities do not, however, constitute a large enough proportion of the PRC population to make such arguments heard. Han Chinese currently constitute 91 percent of the overall population—and, importantly, their numbers do not fall below 50 percent of the overall population in most titular Autonomous Region cities. (Only in rural, mountainous, and remote areas of Autonomous Regions does the Han population fall to between 2 percent and 20 percent of the population.) In contrast, in more than approximately one-quarter of the Indian subcontinent (including the highly populated east-central, northwest, and northeast areas), Hindi speakers constitute less than 50 percent—and, in places, as little as 7 percent—of the total population.

PRC language policies of the early years thus reflected a mixed system, one that officially supported minority languages, yet which yielded less progress than the subsequent decade in changing long-held covert language attitudes against "low quality" non-dominant cultures and languages.

A Model System? Minority-Language Planning, 1980–89

The 1980s were a period of enormous expansion of support for minority languages, with central and local governments establishing and revising writing systems and creating many new language materials and programs. China's language planning system was responsive to local conditions, including in Xinjiang. Yet factors such as negative language attitudes towards minority languages and external events conspired to make the task of fostering minority languages much more difficult.

In 1984, the two most important laws to date on language planning were enacted. The first, Article 46 of the Nationality Law, "guarantees the citizens of every nationality the right to sue in their own nationality spoken and written language in carrying out litigation." Translation was to be provided for those who do not know the relevant language (*Zhonghua... falü huibian* 1985).

Secondly, the *Law on Regional Autonomy* for minority nationalities (which was adopted May 31, 1984, and came into force on Oct. 1 of that year) strengthened rights already present in the 1982 Constitution. Besides encouraging (but not mandating) greater minority representation in Autonomous Region areas, the *Law* stressed increased autonomy in education and culture. Article 38 encouraged literature, arts, news, publishing, broadcasting, films, and television "in nationality form and with the characteristics of the relevant minority." The *Law* also supported the publication of nationality books and the preservation of nationality historical and cultural heritage (id.).

One important development during this period was the establishment of a number of preferential policies (*youhui zhengce*) for minorities, including preferential university entrance requirements.[17] Preferential educational policies proved to be a double-edged sword. While minorities did benefit substantially, such policies also served to confirm the majority's negative stereotypes about the low "quality" of "backward" minorities. These results were unintentional, but they reinforced the very Han chauvinism of which the central government was attempting to extirpate. Despite this persistent sinocentrism, however, the 1980s were characterized by two highly promising developments: the enactment of laws and policies explicitly supporting minority languages, and a significant liberalization of autonomous cultural expression, including language and religion. Such policy liberalization, which was a great stimulus for minority-language education and media, was to last about fifteen years. Thereafter, we witness a backlash against what Beijing perceived as excessive minority cultural autonomy.

How did Uyghur cultural expression come to be seen as "excessive"? Below I explore how the languages of major ethnic groups rival Chinese locally in prestige and power, focusing on the dynamic between policies and their implementation in Xinjiang.

The Status of Languages in Western China

Uyghur as a Lingua Franca

Within China's trend towards monoculturalism, Uyghur constitutes a particularly interesting case study, for as a regional language Uyghur has a significant population of semi-speakers and non-native speakers. Uyghur language policy is also arguably the least stable of that for any minority language in China.

Uyghur is the native language of 8 to 11 million speakers. Conservative estimates place the Xinjiang Uyghur population at 8.4 million (2000 PRC census), with an additional population of 300,000 in Kazakhstan (as of 1993); ca. 90,000 in Kyrgyzstan and Uzbekistan (officially 37,000 in 1998); 3,000 in Afghanistan; and 1,000 in Mongolia (according to a 1982 estimate). Uyghurs have also immigrated to other countries, particularly Turkey, Australia, and Germany.

The language and culture of the Uyghurs is closely related to that of the Uzbeks, though the latter have far more speakers. Both groups are primarily oasis-dwelling and urban farmers and merchants; both speak southeastern Turkic languages and both claim to be the literary heirs to medieval Chagatay culture.[18]

As the Chagatay language was once the lingua franca of much of Central Asia, so now is Uyghur a major interlanguage for nearly 2 million non-Han peoples west of the Gobi desert and east of the Pamir Mountains. These peoples include Tungusic Sibes; Iranic Wakhi and Sarikoli (the latter two officially if erroneously termed "Tajiks"); the Mongolic Dagurs; and even Russians in Xinjiang. Some numerically smaller ethnic minorities in Xinjiang use Uyghur even as their first language. These include Tatars;

Uzbeks; Akto Turks (who are officially Kyrgyz); and some groups lumped under the Uyghur ethnonym, such as the Eynus (exonymically Abdals), Dolans, and Loptuq (exonymically Lopliks). Even major minorities in Xinjiang such as Kazakhs (1.25 million people) and Kyrgyz (0.16 million people), particularly those who reside in or near Uyghur areas, generally have some competence in Uyghur, learning it as a second or third language. Kazakh also constitutes a lingua franca, but only at the prefectural level: In the Ili and Tarbaghatay areas, Kazakh is widely used by minorities lower down on the language hierarchy such as Sibes, Salars, Tatars, and Uzbeks. Still, only Uyghur is a lingua franca for the entire Xinjiang region.

The ethnic diversity of modern Uyghur speakers has had long-term consequences not only for the language, but also for Uyghur culture and identity as well. For example, the bilingual Tatar population of Xinjiang, though small (4,890 in 2000), has in the last century constituted the intellectual vanguard of the Tarim Basin.[19]

As a lingua franca, Uyghur is used in a greater number of social domains than any other language in the area: the home, the marketplace, street and business signs, the media, and in many schools, besides being an official language of government and courts. Local education officials have tacitly supported Uyghur's status as a lingua franca in that the title "Uyghur" is de facto equivalent to "minority nationality" for policymakers and officials. Indeed, for local and national officialdom, the salient ethnolinguistic distinction has been between *Hanzu* ("Han Chinese") and *minzu* ("non-Han").[20] Thus, those Xinjiang institutions—from daycares to universities—that offer both Chinese-language and non-Chinese-language classrooms call Uyghur-language classrooms *minzu ban* ("nationality classes"), even though these classes contain students of mixed ethnicity. Uyghur thus has representative status for the minority languages of Xinjiang, just as Tibetan is the flagship language for greater Tibet.

Situating Major Minority Languages within the Chinese Sphere

The sociolinguistic status of China's languages can be conceptualized as a pyramid, with modern standard Mandarin (*putonghua,* "the common language") at the pyramid's very peak (Dwyer 1998). Below the *National Standard* (Standard Mandarin) in the pyramid are five more levels: *Regional Standards* (or *sub-state languages* (Laponce 1987:115)), including for example Uyghur, Lhasa Tibetan, and regional varieties of Chinese; *Primary Minorities* and *Secondary Minorities* (such as Amdo Tibetan and Evenki,

Figure 1: LANGUAGE AND POWER IN CHINA

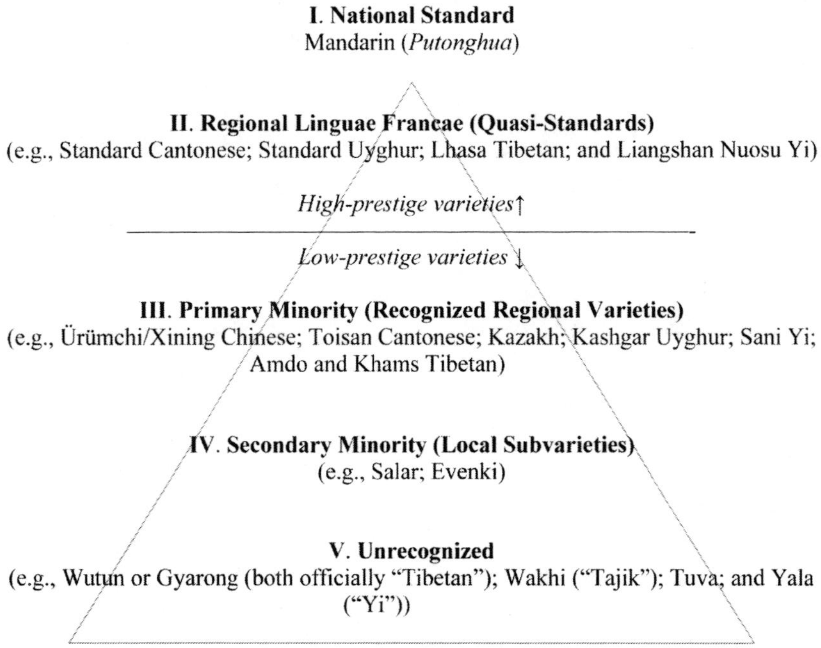

I. National Standard
Mandarin (*Putonghua*)

II. Regional Linguae Francae (Quasi-Standards)
(e.g., Standard Cantonese; Standard Uyghur; Lhasa Tibetan; and Liangshan Nuosu Yi)

High-prestige varieties↑

Low-prestige varieties↓

III. Primary Minority (Recognized Regional Varieties)
(e.g., Ürümchi/Xining Chinese; Toisan Cantonese; Kazakh; Kashgar Uyghur; Sani Yi; Amdo and Khams Tibetan)

IV. Secondary Minority (Local Subvarieties)
(e.g., Salar; Evenki)

V. Unrecognized
(e.g., Wutun or Gyarong (both officially "Tibetan"); Wakhi ("Tajik"); Tuva; and Yala ("Yi"))

respectively); and, finally, *Unrecognized Languages* without official status (e.g., Tuva). See Figure 1 for a spatial rendering of the language-power pyramid.

In terms of prestige and power, regional linguae francae such as Uyghur stand together with Standard Chinese at the top of a sociolinguistic pyramid. Both are high-prestige languages that dominate central institutions including the media and trade on regional and national levels, respectively.

Languages in Levels III–V of the language-power pyramid are low prestige nationally. *Primary* and *Secondary* languages both benefit from preferential language policies, although such policies are often implemented more weakly for *Secondary* languages. While *Primary Minorities* often have access to native-language schooling and broadcast and print media in their languages, *Secondary Minorities* often are not subject to language planning efforts. *Secondary Minorities* with new orthography proposals, for example, do not easily obtain approval from the Nationalities Commission.

Although all ethnolinguistic groups are equal under Chinese law, from a policy standpoint, only the high-prestige language varieties (those in Categories I & II) are accorded language maintenance support. Only varieties with a large population and a significant body of written literature are a focus of language, education, and media policies.

Historically, Chinese elites have considered writing, in particular written Chinese, as the keystone to civilization. Those minority populations with a body of written literature in a non-Latin orthography are accorded significant accommodation by China in administrative, educational, and popular domains. *Regional standards* (III) are the focus of media policy and can control local government, whereas *Local Subvarieties* (IV) and *Unrecognized Languages* (V) are ignored on all but the theoretical level. For local subvarieties and unrecognized languages, the covert monolingual policy of the state eliminates any potential benefits accorded to these languages by the Constitution.

That Category I & II languages have the highest prestige is reflected on modern Chinese paper currency, the *renminbi* (RMB): The reverse side renders the phrase "People's Bank of China" in Chinese, Uyghur, Mongolian, Tibetan, and Zhuang scripts. Minority figures also appear on the obverse of the lower denominations of paper currency; a perky Uyghur woman is depicted on the two *yuan* note.[21] Written Uyghur is thus one of only four minority languages to appear on Chinese currency; the presence of these four minority-script phrases illustrates the relation of writing to high language prestige in China. The presence or absence of a writing system for a language plays a disproportionately large role in the prestige and ultimate success of a given minority language in a nation. Other multilingual nations such as India also feature minority languages on currencies. The Indian rupee features on the obverse the two major standard languages, Hindi and English; the reverse side has fourteen regional minority languages. The absence of an official policy and educational support for the low-prestige language varieties (Categories III–V) reinforces speaker perceptions of the uselessness of their "minor" languages.[22]

The Roots of Modern Language Policy

The Language Standardizing Body

As an indicator of how crucial language is to establishing and maintaining nationhood, a language planning office was opened just months after the CCP established control over Xinjiang. From 1954 to 1986, the official institution for central language planning in Beijing was called the Chinese Committee on Script Reform (*Zhongguo wenzi gaige weiyuan hui*), later renamed the national Language and Script Working Committee (*Guojia yuyan wenzi gongzuo weiyuanhui*).

Its manifestation in Ürümchi, the capital of Xinjiang, was known as the Autonomous Region Language and Script Working Committee (*Aptonom rayonning til-yeziq xizmät komiteti*). It was this committee that employed linguists to reform the region's Arabic-based scripts, especially for Uyghur; the Language and Script Working Committee has branch offices in a number of counties. This committee also published a flagship journal, *Language and Translation*, in the five major languages of Xinjiang: Chinese, Uyghur, Kazak, Kyrgyz, and Oyrat Mongolian. As can be seen from the titles of both the committee and its journal, language planning both in Xinjiang and nationwide was fundamentally equated with orthographic standardization and reform.[23]

State cultural policy... [is] important in defining and reinforcing a particular ethnic identity

State cultural policy, and orthographic policy in particular, becomes important in defining and reinforcing a particular ethnic identity. In Xinjiang, script changes, in-migration of Chinese, and heavy long-term intercultural contact has resulted in the Uyghur ethnic group constantly redefining itself, increasingly in opposition to the Chinese.

Orthographies

Although the descriptions below of the many orthographic reforms over the centuries may seem excessively detailed, the reforms mirror changes in Uyghur identity. Scripts index Uyghur identity, even though writing systems alone are but one small part of ethnic identities. Arabic-script Uyghur, for example, indexes two crucial features of modern Uyghur identity: the Turkic Uyghur language, and being Muslim. Having gone through so many writing systems (chosen or imposed) is one important way that the Uyghurs of Xinjiang differ from their Inner Asian neighbors. Tibetan identities, for example, have arguably been more constant over time, reinforced by the continuous use of one Tibetan orthography since the 7th century.

Through two millennia, the Tarim Basin has played host to over two-dozen writing systems representing a variety of orthographic types: Sinitic logographic-ideographic scripts (e.g., Chinese or Kitan); Aramaic alphabetic scripts (e.g., Sogdian (Old) Uyghur, later adopted and successively standardized by the Mongols);[24] and syllabic writing systems like Brahmi (e.g., Khotanese), among others. The diversity of orthographies in the area attests to the syncretic effects of extensive long-term exchange across Eurasia to the Indian subcontinent—exchange not merely of goods, but also of religion and language. Indeed, many writing systems were associated with particular religions when introduced into the area: the Sogdian script with Nestorian Christianity, the 'Phags pa script with Tibetan Buddhism, Arabic with Islam, and (some would argue) Cyrillic with Soviet-style communism. By the early 20th century, Arabic-based Turkic and Chinese were the two most common orthographies in the Tarim Basin.

Orthographic Reform

In the 20th century, Cyrillic and Latin-based scripts were introduced alongside the surviving Arabic-based orthographies and Chinese. Before 1949, the question of a "Chinese language policy" in Inner Asia is moot: Those ruling the vast territory we today call China had no hand in the adoption and reformation of writing systems there.

Sogdian-script Mongolian

Historically, orthographic standardization in Inner Asia was largely confined to the Mongols. From the 13th century at the beginning of the Mongol Yuan dynasty to the 17th century, Mongols employed the Sogdian script adopted from the historical Uyghurs. They also used the ill-suited Chinese orthography to write Mongolian.[25] Under Khubilai Khan, the Mongols took a 99-year orthographic detour. Reigning over China and Inner Asia, Khubilai Khan saw the need to have a new script developed that adequately represented the major languages of his empire, and had a high-ranking Tibetan Buddhist lama 'Phags pa develop a new Sanskrit and Tibetan-based script in 1269. Though it was decreed official, the 'Phags pa script (*dörbeljin üsüg*, "square writing") never came into widespread use and was abandoned with the fall of the Yuan dynasty in 1368.

The Sogdian Mongol script, in continuous use since the 13th century, was substantially revised for Oyrat (western Mongolian) in the mid-17th century by the Oyrat leader and Lama Zaya Pandita. This revision, termed *todo bichig* ("clear writing") eliminated ambiguities in Sogdian script Mongolian. The latter unrevised and older *hudum* script also remained in use and was mandated for some schools in Xinjiang and Inner Mongolia from the 1970s to 1990s. In the mid-1990s, the *hudum* script was centrally mandated as the standard for written Mongolian across China. Since 1941, the Republic of Mongolia used a modified Cyrillic standard orthography based on the Soviet model to write standard Khalkha Mongolian. Since the mid-1990s, however, the country has also been reviving the Sogdian-based *hudum* script.

Such script unification is not without obstacles, however: The vertical *hudum* script is more difficult to learn than a Latin- or Cyrillic-based script, as it contains a number of homographs (front and back vowels are not distinguished, nor are voiced and voiceless stops), and each glyph has three forms (initial, medial, and final). Furthermore, as with Tibetan, the *hudum* script reflects a much older variety of the language, so that many written glyphs are not pronounced. None of these obstacles is insurmountable; after all, English has managed to become an international language despite having an infamously archaic and irregular spelling system; Arabic-based scripts like those used in Xinjiang also have up to four forms of each character. If the transition from Cyrillic to a Sogdian-based script were successfully implemented in Mongolia, this standardization would allow most Mongols a unified orthography, unlike the Turkic speakers of Inner and Central Asia.

Experiments with Cyrillic-based orthographies
In the 1920s and 1930s, as Central Asia came under Soviet control, all of the Central Asian Soviet republics were required to adopt diverse Cyrillic orthographies. These republics also discussed developing writing systems for the sizeable Central Asian Uyghur population as well, though Uyghur was to be one of the last Central Asian Turkic languages to adopt Cyrillic.[26]

The decades following the foundation of the PRC saw a period of orthographic chaos for major Inner Asian languages within the Chinese sphere, with language planning flapping along behind ever-shifting political winds. Between 1949 and 1957, Chinese language policy was closely tied to that of the Soviet Union. Though Cyrillic-based Uyghur had already been approved in the Soviet Central Asian republics in 1946, re-standardization of even the Arabic-based Uyghur script was approved first on Soviet territory (Almaty) in 1951. This standard was then adopted on the advice of Soviet advisors for China's new Xinjiang Uygur Autonomous Region in 1954.[27]

Usage of Cyrillic in Xinjiang reached its peak between 1955 and

1958, when it was introduced into a number of schools and employed in academic publications. Actual policy, however, was chaotic, with Cyrillic officially adopted in 1956, officially abandoned in February 1957, and then reinstated later that year.

Arabic-based Turkic orthographies

For the oasis dwellers of the Tarim and Junggarian Basins, an Arabic-based script gradually became dominant between the 10th and 15th centuries as Islam spread eastwards in the region. Before being adopted east of the Pamirs, this script had been adapted for Persian much earlier and then had been modified for the medieval Central Asian Turkic lingua franca Chagatay. This orthography has predominated in the region up to the present day.

The Arabic-based script was first revised for Uyghur in 1925.[28] From 1930 to 1946, Uyghurs in the Soviet sphere used both the official Latin-based script and an unofficial Cyrillic script for Uyghur, adopting Cyrillic officially only in 1946. East of the Pamirs, where there had been no official change to a Latin-based script, the Arabic-based script continued to be used. Even in the border areas of Ili and Tarbaghatay, the Latin script had not taken hold. Instead, a standardization of the Uyghur Arabic script was proposed by the Uyghur linguist Ibrahim Muti in Ürümchi in 1948. In 1979, the Old Script (*kona yeziq*, i.e., Arabic-based) was revived. 1982 and 1987 saw the formal adoption of a revised version of the 1920s Arabic script. Pamphlets and an orthographic dictionary were then published first to facilitate the transition and then to promulgate the latest orthographic reform of the early 1990s (Xinjiang UAR Language and Script Task Committee 1985).

Nearly all Uyghurs favor the Arabic script for reasons of practicality, aesthetics, and group identity. Knowledge of this script allows access to the largest body of modern Uyghur and premodern Central Asian literature. The Arabic script is considered by Uyghurs to be beautiful; indeed, it is also an important art form. (In contrast, one could hardly imagine calligraphy in *pinyin*.) However, it is Arabic script's fundamental association with Islam that is the crucial argument in its favor: Although many

being Muslim Turkic is central to a modern Uyghur ethnic identity

(particularly northern) Uyghurs are secularized, being Muslim Turkic is central to a modern Uyghur ethnic identity. Being Muslim distinguishes the Uyghurs from the Hans and all other non-Muslim peoples; while being

Turkic speakers distinguishes them from the Chinese-speaking Muslims (known as *Dunggans* or *Hui*).[29]

Experiments with Latin-based orthographies

Since the establishment of the People's Republic, however, systematic planning efforts for the country's languages had been implemented, including the introduction of a Latin-based transliteration system known as *pinyin*. After the relationship between China and the Soviet Union had completely soured, the Latin-script-based *pinyin* system replaced Cyrillic for the major Turkic languages of Xinjiang: Uyghur, Kazakh, and later, for Kyrgyz. In the case of Inner Mongolia, Premier Zhou Enlai intervened personally to ensure the switch from the Russian-associated Cyrillic script to a Chinese-associated *pinyin* Latin script, which had been developed in the 1950s for the analphabetic masses as a stepping-stone to Chinese characters.[30]

In Xinjiang, this so-called *yengi yeziq* ("New Script") was taught on a trial basis in some primary schools starting in the 1960s, and came into wider use in 1974.[31] Both Arabic- and Latin-based scripts were used concomitantly for about a decade, although those literate in Arabic-script Uyghur and Kazakh were quite reluctant to use the New Script. Nonetheless, the Language and Script Committee formally adopted the new Latin-based script in August 1976. In 1978, this orthography was employed by all the mass media as well as a reported 70 percent of intellectuals and 50 percent of the general citizenry (Jarring 1986: 31). Some books continued to be published in *yengi yeziq* after the Cultural Revolution, especially reprints such as the excellent Uyghur-Chinese dictionary (*Uyghurchä-Hänzuchä lughät*) published by Xinjiang Renmin press (1979/1982).[32]

The latinization of Chinese minority languages has a precedent, of course, in the latinization of Han Chinese in the early 20th century. Modern Chinese has been very resistant to foreign incursion. The foreign dynasties of China—e.g., the Mongol Yuan and the Manchu Qing—did not succeed in usurping Chinese and establishing their language as the standard. During the early 20th century, the colloquializing *baihua* movement included discussions of adopting a Latin-based script in order to "modernize" Chinese. Though latinization was inspired by contact with the West, most policymakers never seriously entertained the notion of replacing Chinese characters by a Latin script. Still, a handful of materials were produced in the late 1920s, with the aim of using the script as a bridge to Chinese characters.[33] These materials may well have constituted a precursor to the Latin-based scripts (such as Uyghur *yengi yeziq*) for the Turkic languages of Xinjiang.

Broader implications

Languages with orthographies have political clout and emotional resonance. People become invested in reading and writing in a particular script, and attempts to make changes often sparks resistance. Early on, the central PRC government recognized the importance of orthographic planning. The frequent script changes from the 1950s through the 1980s unfortunately cut off an entire generation of Uyghurs from the large corpus of literature and history in the Arabic script written prior to 1950, as well as from written communication with those much younger or older who had been educated in an Arabic-based script (Li 1953, Osmanov 1987, Wali 1986, and Jarring 1981). Pupils and students who were in the school system at any time from 1950 to 1976 were subject to these changes.

The return to Arabic-based script in the early 1980s coincided with a gradual relaxation of restrictions on minority religion and language, arguably the two most central expressions of culture and identity. The Arabic orthography was and is closely tied to the recovery of Uyghur ethnic heritage. This heritage had been lost in both a concrete and a conceptual sense. During the chaos of the Cultural Revolution, hundreds of thousands of books and old manuscripts were removed from libraries and private homes and

> *uniquely Uyghur heritage [has been] recast as part of a Chinese historical narrative*

destroyed, as they were across China. What constituted uniquely *Uyghur* heritage was recast as part of a *Chinese* historical narrative: Uyghur heritage was no longer a coherent, conceptually independent whole, but rather had become one small branch on the tree of the great Chinese nation. Across China, reducing hundreds of ethnic histories, identities, and languages to the same simple categories and trajectories was seen by the new central government as crucial in building national unity. Upon meeting with Ürümchi scholars in 1978, former Ambassador Gunnar Jarring noted dryly: "Culture and science were represented by two Han-Chinese, three Uighur men, and one Uighur woman—all employees of the Urumchi university in different capacities. The two Chinese were responsible for history."[34]

Transnational considerations

While Uyghurs have generally looked westwards towards Transoxiana for a contextualization of their ethnic identity, the PRC requires them to look eastward in order to build national unity. Though Chinese historiography of the country's minority nationalities has been constant and predictable, China's language-planning efforts have been ideologically and pragmatically chaotic. The experiments with Cyrillic- and Latin-based scripts were associated with communist ideology (one Soviet, the other Chinese); their rejection in favor of the Arabic-based orthography can be seen both as an acknowledgement of failure and as an important concession to Turkic-speaking Muslim identity—i.e., Uyghur, Kazakh, and Kyrgyz. *Yengi yeziq* evoked both Chinese and Western languages, to which Uyghur is unrelated. Even though many Turkic speakers in western China are secular, Islam is central to ethnic identity.

Since 1989, the PRC government has had an additional motivation to support Arabic-script Turkic. Within a few years of independence from the Soviet Union, three of the Central Asian republics—Azerbayjan, Uzbekistan, and Turkmenistan—moved to switch from Cyrillic to Latin-based alphabets. "The impetus...was perceived as an instrument of de-sovietization and at the same time as a means of individual nation-building, westernization, and modernization" (Landau and Kellner-Heinkele 2001). Kyrgyzstan and Kazakhstan (with larger Russian populations than the other republics) along with Tajikistan opted to continue using Cyrillic alphabets, though the Kyrgyz Republic is also slowly adopting a Latin-based script as well.

That Uyghurs, Kazakhs, and Kyrgyz on the Chinese side of the border had been using the Arabic script since 1979 became a boon for Chinese nation building, since the orthographic differences across the border created a psychological and practical barrier to inter-Turkic communication in Central Asia. The unique use in Central Asia of an Arabic-based script by Xinjiang's Uyghurs, Kazakhs, and Kyrgyz focused the language-issue discussion inwards and towards Beijing. Thus, both for central government policymakers and for Turkic speakers of Xinjiang, the Arabic-script policy can be said to be a success. Paradoxically, the policy discourages contact with Cyrillic-Turkic Central Asia, yet fosters a Turkic Islamic identity. Use of the Sogdian script for Mongolic languages like Oyrat and Khalkha has the same emotional effect of reconnecting the Mongols with their past (in their case, with the heroic days of Genghis and Khubilai Khan).

Technology-driven innovations: a new Latin-based standard?
Internet use in China is growing by leaps and bounds. Between 1998 and 1999 alone, the number of Internet users in China increased 322 percent—

by far the largest increase by any nation during that period.[35] Internet cafes are the most common Internet access points in China, although students frequent university computer labs. These cafes are now commonplace in cities and towns, and tend to be segregated by ethnicity (some for Hans, others for Uyghurs, and still others for foreigners). Cities such as Kashgar, Ürümchi, Ili/Ghulja, Keriyä, Korla, and Hami/Qumul all have multiple Internet cafes that are frequented by young people (largely males). Access to and use of these cafes, as elsewhere in China, is strictly monitored, and a number of websites are blocked. Nationwide, at least 30,000 government employees are involved in monitoring Internet traffic, and the computer science department of Xinjiang University provides training for those who need to decode messages in Uyghur. Doing so is considered a matter of national security.

Despite the close monitoring, Internet use (web browsing, e-mail, gaming, and participating in chat rooms and listservs) is enthusiastic. The advent of Internet communications has also stimulated the adaptation of Latin-based orthographies to transliterate Uyghur; these orthographies have been dubbed *Uyghur kompyuter yeziqi* or *Uyghur Internet yeziqi* ("Uyghur computer/Internet orthography"). During Internet discussions in the mid-1990s, Uyghur speakers debated a quasi-standard orthography based on phonetic transcription, Turkish, or Chinese *pinyin* transliteration. No consensus has been reached to date. Some users, particularly those educated in Chinese schools, find *pinyin*'s economical use of the keyboard intuitive. Any citizen of China educated since 1957 can also sound out *pinyin* quickly. The very glyphs that make *pinyin* compact, however, are hard to decipher for anyone educated outside the People's Republic (particularly *x* for *š* as in *Xinjiang* and *q* for *č* as in *Qinghai*). However, some Xinjiang Internet users avoid *pinyin* as a matter of ethnic identity: For some, *pinyin* smacks of Chineseness.[36]

Internet discussion forums overwhelmingly support the use of a Latin-based script for computer-based communication, but participants express mixed opinions about changing the official script in Xinjiang. One essayist, citing an article from the *Xinjiang Daily* in March 2003, stated that, while he found the *yengi yeziq* Latin script indispensable for transcription and transliteration, Arabic-script Uyghur was equally worth employing for other purposes (Ershidin 2003, Erdem 2003).

Latin-script Uyghur is in any case extremely popular in the computing domain. Within the next decade, either an official or a *de facto* standard for Latin-script computing Uyghur will likely be established. If an official standard is promulgated, it is likely to be *pinyin*-based. If *de facto* standards emerge, they will likely be more codified versions of current Internet usage—one modeled on the Central Asian Latin scripts, and the other based on *pinyin*. The former asserts Uyghur identity as distinct from that of the Chinese; the latter is readily learnable by anyone educated in Chinese schools.

Computing Standardization, Research, and Development

Technology is in large part driving the current surge in Latin-script Uyghur use. Since the simplest forms of Latin-script Uyghur are lower ASCII (keyboard) characters, no special computer programs or fonts are required to scan, type, or structure Latin-script Uyghur data.[37] The data can thus be typed anywhere with any operating system. Arabic-script computing, on the other hand, requires (a) a program rendering the script in a right-to-left orientation; (b) the remapping of non-Arabic keyboards; and (c) for Uyghur, specially modified Arabic fonts. (Typically these are modified Persian typefaces of Arabic fonts.) Optical character recognition of scanned Arabic-script materials is still in development, and is not yet available for Uyghur. These current hindrances to Arabic serve to boost Latin-script usage in the short term. Within a decade, however, Arabic-script Uyghur computing will be convenient enough to be employed by a large number of users, if current trends continue.

Since the early 1990s,[38] computer scientists in Xinjiang have localized and upgraded a variety of commercial and noncommercial software. Starting with add-on keyboarding utilities for Arabic-script Uyghur, they have since developed desktop publishing tools (generally as add-ons to Microsoft Office, but also to Photoshop); modified operating systems (DOS, Windows, Linux); and created new tools such as *Tarjiman* (a translation tool), *al Katip* (word-processing software), and *al Korrector* (a spell-checking utility). Beginning in the mid-1990s, software engineers formed commercial enterprises to market their software. There is even a Uyghur-language computer magazine, *Kompyuter Dunyasi* (*Computer World*).

The overwhelming majority of these initiatives came from within Xinjiang, principally from Ürümchi, rather than from Beijing: Of 34 tools, only five were developed in Beijing between 1990 and 1993. All others were developed in Xinjiang: Ürümchi (28) and Aqsu (1). The main impetus behind such innovations was Xinjiang University and its affiliates (which developed 13 of the tools); after 1995, software innovation has been primarily in the hands of private companies, which have developed 11 such tools as of 2001 (Sugawara 2001: 24). This trend towards private initiatives will only continue, with a wide range of commercial and non-commercial products expected to be available in the coming year. Mobile phone service is also available with a Uyghur interface. Such developments point to the vitality of Xinjiang's information technology climate.

Internationally, there are also initiatives to standardize computer encoding for Arabic-script Uyghur, Kazakh, and Kyrgyz. Since 1995, volunteers have been working on an ISO (International Organization for Standardization) proposal for these languages (ISO 1995). Without such standardization, data exchange is hampered. In 2000, China supported these international standardizing bodies for computing encoding (the ISO/IEC and the Unicode Consortium) by publishing a Chinese national standard, GB 13000. The latter (since updated) was compatible with the now-worldwide standard of ISO 10646, better known as Unicode.[39] GB 13000 and its successors specified code points for four major minority languages of China: Arabic-script Uyghur, Sogdian-script Mongolian, Tibetan, and Yi, as well as for the languages heretofore supported by Unicode (including Chinese, Japanese, and Korean (CJK) characters). GB 18030 support became mandatory for all operating systems sold in Mainland China on September 1, 2001 (Fok 2002). The domestic and international research and development in informatics provides ample proof that Uyghur is a major world language.

The Politics of Creating Standard Uyghur

Central to the process of standardization is the selection and codification of one prestige language variety. Far from being a simple process of sorting through all dialects and picking the one with the biggest population, standard dialect candidates are inevitably associated with the elite stratum of a given society. Only then can a dialect be elevated to the status of a language. We therefore must update Max Weinreich's oft-quoted observation that "a language is a dialect with an army and a navy"[40] to Tove Skutnabb-Kangas' proposition that "a language is a dialect promoted by elites" (Skutnabb-Kangas 1997–2004, Phillipson 1988).

Standardization involves developing a norm that overrides regional dialects, a process that then allows specific linguistic contexts to be evaluated and codified. Both Standard Uyghur of China and the Uyghur spoken in the former Soviet Union have undergone language-planning normalization. Both norms are based on northern dialects: Xinjiang's is based on the regional capital dialect of Ürümchi plus that of the Ili Valley bordering Kazakhstan; in Kazakhstan, the standard is simply based on the Ili Valley dialect as spoken in Kazakhstan. Differences between the two standards exist mainly in the lexical realm and are attributable to the influence of different dominant languages (Chinese versus Russian).

Uyghur comprises all the language varieties spoken by sedentary Turkic speakers in the major oases and Tian Shan foothill towns of Xinjiang: those in the north and center (Ürümchi, Ili, Korla); the east (Qumul (Hami), and Turfan); the east-central area (Lop Nur); and the south (Aqsu, Kashgar, and Hotän (Khotan)). Of the 8.4 million Uyghurs in Xinjiang, more than half are speakers of Standard Uyghur, which largely overlaps with Central Uyghur. The language of northern Xinjiang including the Ili Valley and the regional capital Ürümchi forms the basis for the standard language. By most scholars' accounts, Central Uyghur also includes Turfan and Hami. There is, however, some disagreement as to how to divide the language varieties of southern Xinjiang. The prevailing view is that the area of Hotän and environs in the south constitutes one dialect area; that Kashgar, Atush, and environs in the southwest constitute another; and that Lop Nor (with 25,000 speakers), in the east-central area, is an isolated dialect island.[41]

Yet population and geography also played a role in the standardization of Uyghur. Although the south has often been considered the spiritual and cultural Uyghur center, the Uyghur population, resources (both natural and economic), and political-administrative centers are all concentrated in the north. Income levels in the south are far below those of the north. A contributing factor to this disparity is the harsher, more arid climate in the south, whose ecology cannot support large populations. Moreover, illiteracy is especially high in the rural southern Tarim Basin, where most Uyghurs are impoverished farmers. Not surprisingly, these factors conspired to guarantee that this northern variety of modern Uyghur would constitute the basis of the standard language.

Language Modernization

Language Attitudes and Early Modernization

For long-term viability, a language must be made an appropriate communication medium for modern topics and discourse forms. Beginning in the late 1950s, the XUAR Language and Script Committee, in addition to reforming the orthography, made efforts to modernize the lexicon. The committee was given the task to standardize the extant lexicon as well as to introduce neologisms from Chinese (see, for example, Yunus 1996). Nationwide, regional language planners also introduced and standardized socialist political vocabulary for minority languages.

For Uyghur, the percentages of lexemes of Turkic, Arabic, Persian, and Russian origin were carefully noted. Citing percentages of loan words became *de rigueur* even for non-lexicological academic writings on the Uyghur language. These frequent citations were irritating to many Uyghur intellectuals, who found them insulting. "It made it sound as though Uyghur wasn't a real language, but rather a patchwork of foreign words thrown together," complained one Uyghur academic in 1991.

New lexical items—particularly in political and technical areas—were adopted. Already common terms previously introduced from Russian (such as *poyiz* ("train"), *ayiroplan* ("airplane"), and *üstäl* ("table") were augmented with administrative-political terms (*fakultet*—"academic department"). But with the departure of Soviet advisors in the late 1950s, people in Inner Asia were no longer exposed to the Russian language through schools and the media. The new language of modern science and administration in Xinjiang was suddenly Chinese. As the Kazakhstan Uyghur linguist É. Nadzip wrote in 1970, Chinese words were "being introduced in a compulsory manner as a result of the official language policy and...numerous Chinese words in the realm of sociopolitical, scientific-technological, and other terminology are infiltrating the language by dislodging Uigur, Arabic, Persian, and Russian words" (Bruchis 1988: 221).

The undeniable increase in Chinese loan words into Uyghur that began in the 1960s, however, had as much to do with Han Chinese in-migration and geopolitics as with deliberate language policy. Over the course of 40 years, as Chinese engineers, teachers, and traders settled in Inner Asia— particularly in Inner Mongolia and Xinjiang—local people had much more exposure to the Chinese language than ever before. Certainly the media and the schools played a crucial role in introducing scientific, technological, and administrative terms from Chinese. Eventually, learning these terms would become crucial to the economic livelihood of Chinese minorities.

Yet language planners in Xinjiang were never overly preoccupied with language purism. In marked contrast to the Turkish Language Society, which in Turkey was charged with replacing Arabic and Persian elements in modern Turkish with "Turkic" constructions, the Xinjiang Language and Script Committee never had a mandate to "cleanse" Uyghur. Rather, demographic and economic pressures have resulted in the adoption into Uyghur of terms from Russian, Chinese, and English. The lack of a strong mandate to modernize and expand vocabulary of major Inner Asian languages, however, meant that Uyghur, Mongolian, and Tibetan would inevitably fall behind Chinese in their ability to express concepts of modern technology and communications.

Neologisms

All languages can potentially be used for technical purposes. But when a language lacks technical terminology, however, a well-funded planning organization is necessary to create, standardize, and disseminate neologisms in the language. Just across the border, Kazakhstan is demonstrating that such planning can have a marked effect on a region's language in a relatively short period of time. The success of Kazakhstan's efforts is abetted by the post-independence enthusiasm of Kazakh intellectuals and even ordinary people there for language development.

But in Xinjiang, regionalism and a plethora of sizeable ethnic groups have historically diluted any potential support for Uyghur language development. Some Uyghur intellectuals have pushed for a limited linguistic purism: To strengthen Uyghur ethnic identity and stem the flow of Chinese words and structures into the Uyghur language, these analysts proposed to create neologisms from Turkic roots or to revive words from an earlier stage of the language. However, although a handful of Turkic neologisms were indeed introduced, many proved far more cumbersome than their Chinese equivalents—for example, the Neo-Uyghur term *tonglatghu mashinisi* (literally, "freezing machine") for "refrigerator." (I have yet to meet a Xinjiang Uyghur who uses anything but the far briefer Chinese term *bingxiang*.) Similarly, in Sichuan Yi, "school" has been rendered as *ssodde* (literally, "learning place"); yet in conversation, one hears only Sichuan Chinese *xioxiao* ("school").[42] When it comes to the lexicon, practicality trumps ideology.

Official language policy in Xinjiang was subject to reversals, and a number of new terms were created for Uyghur, Kazakh, and Kyrgyz, particularly during the political and cultural liberalization of the 1980s. These terms tended to compete with Chinese loan words. Yet less than a decade later, journal editors were subject to regulations that required neologisms to be introduced from Chinese, not from English or Russian

(1991 interview, Light 1998b).

Throughout Inner and Central Asia, speakers of minority languages support coining or reviving indigenous terms to counterbalance the perceived excess of dominant-language vocabulary. Thus, Kazakhstan introduced Turkic *egemendik* for Russian *suverenitet* ("sovereignty"); in Turkmenistan, Turkic *otly* was introduced for Russian *poezd* ("train"); and in Uzbekistan, Arabic and Persian *tajjoragoh* substituted for Russian *aeroport* ("airport"). In the Central Asian republics, however, loan words from Western languages (e.g., English *biznes*) have also been readily adopted (Schlyter 2001).

The functions of the Xinjiang Language and Script Committee have broadened considerably from its original overt mission of developing a language norm, standardizing an orthography, and instituting language codification. Today, the committee is far more active in the public sphere—fostering political, educational, media, and public service working groups and even an informative website (Xinjiang Uyghur Autonomous Regional Working Committee of Minorities' Language and Writing. 2004).

Covert Policy: Diluting Culture

Monism (Monoculturalism/Monolingualism)
Beginning in the 1980s, China enacted minority cultural policies that were at once accommodationist and assimilative.[43] As China relaxed restrictions on religious expression and fostered minority-language materials, it simultaneously expanded efforts to dilute minority culture. Both the accommodationist and the assimilationist trends occurred in the important language domains of education and the media.

> *minority cultural policies…were at once accomodationist and assimilative*

Such an apparent policy paradox is readily interpretable if we understand it as the simultaneous implementation of overt and covert policy. China's covert language policy was to become ever more *monist*, i.e., reducing linguistic diversity to one colonialist principle of statehood (Schiffman 1999). The rationale for such policies may have been for the economic benefit of all citizens of the Chinese nation, but the net effect has been a steady march towards a monocultural and monolingual nation through the economic, political, and cultural integration of the peoples on its peripheries.

This assimilationist trend created an overarching national identity (*Zhongguo ren,* "person of China"), thereby diluting the individual identities of its minorities. In China's West, a new non-ethnic identity, *Xinjiang ren* ("New Territorian," i.e., "a person of Xinjiang") has been consciously created and promulgated in the media, to particularly good effect in pop songs. Many Hans in the region now call themselves *Xinjiang ren*. The large increases in the Xinjiang Han population over the last decade have even prompted debates over whether the ethnonym *Uygur* should be deleted from the administrative toponym "Xinjiang Uygur Autonomous Region." Aside from its effective withdrawal of recognition for the region's titular ethnic group, such a move would have serious implications for the allocation of resources, particularly education funding.

Linguistics in the Service of Monist Politics

Pan-Turkism

Language families are ascertained by systematically comparing modern language varieties, as well as by reconstructing earlier stages of the language family. Via decades and centuries of applying this so-called historical-comparative method, scholars have established groups of related languages, or language families, such as Indo-European or Sino-Tibetan. Languages are assigned by scholars to the same family when they display systematic correspondences of linguistic features. Though some hypotheses (particularly for macrofamilies) have triggered disagreement, in general, theories of language relationships are widely accepted by scholars.

Uyghur, Kazakh, and Kyrgyz are part of the Turkic language family. Given that the modern border was historically porous, there is little difference between the forms of these languages spoken in Xinjiang and those of the respective titular Central Asian republics.[44] Besides a high degree of mutual intelligibility, Uyghurs and other groups east and west of the Pamir Mountains share similar though not identical cultural identities. Yet beyond this intragroup identity (e.g., Kazakhstan/Xinjiang Uyghur), a degree of overlapping identities between groups also exists. For example, the Uzbeks, Uyghurs, and Kyrgyz all claim Mahmud al-Kashgari, the well-known 11th century scholar, as their own.

But for modern China, which advertises itself domestically and internationally as a "unitary multi-ethnic Chinese nation" (PRC Embassy 2004), transnational linguistic solidarities are potentially threatening to the concept of nationhood. Uniting the "multi-ethnic" Chinese nation requires its citizenry to consider itself "unitary," or part of one national identity (*Zhongguo ren*, "person of China") under which individual ethnic identities are clearly subordinate.

transnational linguistic solidarities are potentially threatening to the concept of nationhood

Thus any language families spanning China's international borders are potentially problematic. Turkic is a case in point: Although the collocation *Tujue yuzu* ("Turkic language family") alone was acceptable in official discourse until at least 1996, under no circumstances was the adjective *Tujue* allowed to be used in any other context. Also forbidden (as indicated by the following asterisks) were for example the phrases *Tujue wenhua* ("Turkic culture") and *Tujue ren* ("Turkic person"). To the authorities in Beijing, the idea that Kazakhs, Kyrgyz, Uyghurs, Tatars, and Uzbeks could all consider themselves Turkic is no doubt alarming. In the view of CCP leaders, calling oneself "Turkic" is the first step down the slippery slope to the dreaded pan-Turkism heralded from the Bosporus to South Siberia. So there is officially no such Turkic ethnicity, only a linguistic one ("Turkic language family"), and even this term has fallen out of favor since 1996.

From 1993 to 1996, the Central Nationalities Institute (now Central Nationalities University) in Beijing did have a Department of Turkology. "Turkology" in China generally refers to the linguistic description of the Turkic languages located within the current borders of the People's Republic. Elsewhere in the world, however, the field of Turkology encompasses not just linguistics but also literature, politics, history, and the arts, and is focused on most of Eurasia, from Manchuria to the Bosporus.) After 1996, however, this Turkology faculty (*Tujueyu xi*, "Turkic Languages Faculty") came to be called the *Minyu er xi* ("Two Ethnic Languages Faculty" or "Uyghur-Kazakh Faculty"), leaving out Xinjiang Kyrgyz and all the other Turkic languages. Since April 2000, even the *Minyu er xi* has been split into a "Uyghur department" and a tiny "Kazak department."

Such labels suggest that Uyghur and Kazakh are two autonomous unrelated languages; indeed, the terms define two of the 56 nationalities that China has placed under the unifying rubric *Zhongguo ren* ("person of China"). Tertiary institutions with instruction in the languages and literatures of the regional minorities (e.g., Xinjiang University) have faculties entitled *Zhongyu xi* ("Languages of China Department") and *Zhongyu wenxue xi* ("Literatures of the Languages of China Department").

In contrast, the Central Asian republics have since 1989 considered cultural pan-Turkism an asset. The similar Latin scripts being introduced in most Central Asian republics create the possibility of a regional pan-Turkic cultural identity. For the Central Asian republics, the practicality of a Turkish-style Latin script outweighed other considerations: The script is easy to type and allows some degree of communication between all the states in the region as well as with Turkey. The absence of an Arabic script standard may also be due to the secularization of governmental policymakers there, who felt no allegiance to Islam.

In China, official resistance to pan-Turkism encompasses not just political but also cultural realms, even though script reform has not produced significant political solidarity between the Central Asian republics. First, rightly or wrongly, the public perception in Xinjiang is that the slight orthographic differences between the Uyghur, Kazakh, and Kyrgyz Arabic scripts were an intentional divide and conquer tactic. Secondly, there is a covert prohibition in PRC academia of comparative research *within* language families. Researchers avoid studying etymologies of related languages lest the evidence they uncover point to hypothesizing a new language grouping. Secondly, in their analyses of ethnolinguistic groups located both within and outside of China's borders, scholars avoid including relevant data from these languages in neighboring countries. Thus, a grammar of *Miao* (a Chinese ethnonym for a number of related groups) contains no mention of the subgroups Hmong and Mien in, for example, Thailand and Laos. Also, a college textbook on comparative Turkic linguistics (Li 1992) has no mention of the main region—Central Asia—where Turkic languages are spoken; moreover, the Turkic language-family classification is reprinted from that of foreign scholars, so that scholars in China need not risk putting their names to such a dangerously transnational theory (Dwyer 1998). This concerted effort to hinder knowledge about the scientific connections between language families across borders encourages minority-language speakers and researchers to look eastwards to Beijing.

The concomitant rise of contrastive linguistics
The haven of contrastive linguistics has long been a safe port for bored Soviet linguists in the former USSR; now it seems that Chinese linguists are all docking their ships there as well. Innumerable contrastive grammars of minority languages and Standard Chinese are being

written, with the express aim of improving minority learning of the national language. The increase in contrastive studies is directly related to the politicization of linguistics, for as topics such as etymology become dangerous, the only way to conduct research on minority languages is to anchor these studies in Chinese. In effect, the only kind of linguistic research on minority languages that is now acceptable is applied linguistics (language pedagogy and materials development)—all in the service of Chinese as a second language.

Han Chinese-language competence in Uyghur

Article 49 of the Law on Regional Autonomy states that "cadres of Han nationality should learn the spoken and written languages of the local minority nationalities" (Zhongguo...zizhifa 2001: 55). In practice, however, hardly any Hans learn more than *yaxshimusiz* ("hello") in Uyghur. The flaccid official efforts to raise Chinese competence in the Uyghur language have arisen largely for their entertainment value or out of a sense of noblesse oblige. One example of this dynamic can be found in the brief television broadcasts "One Sentence a Week" (*Mei zhou yi ju hua*) and their companion book. These ten-minute broadcasts featured a prominent and engaging Uyghur linguist who gamely repeated one sentence—such as "I am very pleased to meet you"—in standard Uyghur and then again (and again) in perfect Mandarin Chinese for the entire ten-minute segment.[45] Though a noble effort on the part of the producers, motivated learners needed much more structured and systematic exposure to the language. While excellent Chinese-Uyghur textbooks have been available since the 1980s (Mätniyaz and In'amshah 1991, Yi and Gao 1991), only a handful of Han university students have taken the opportunity to learn Uyghur.[46]

Linguistic nationalism or educational reform? The rise of the HSK tests

In 1990, the Beijing Language and Culture University developed the first standardized test for assessing the Chinese competence of non-native speakers: the HSK (*Hanyu shuiping kaoshi*—"Chinese competence test"). The HSK test has been put to use largely for the assessment and "encouragement" of non-native speakers of Chinese.[47] In 1992, the Education Commission announced a plan to implement regular HSK assessment in national minority schools; and a 1997 document specified that a trial assessment of the test would occur between 1998 and 2000 in schools in Xinjiang, Inner Mongolia, Qinghai, and Jilin (Education Commission 1997, cited in Bilik n.d.). HSK tests are now being used as a requirement for minority advancement at some historically minority universities (such as Xinjiang University). Only achieving a minimum score on an HSK test can guarantee academic promotion.

China-wide, HSK tests are both pragmatic and nationalistic. They are pragmatic in that an American-style standardized multiple-choice test should theoretically allow for a fair, countrywide assessment, including of foreign students. The test is clearly an imitation of the Test of English as a Foreign Language (TOEFL). HSK is also patently nationalistic, showing that Chinese universities have high standards and demonstrating China's newfound pride in Chinese as a world language fully competitive with English. The absence of equivalent standardized tests (e.g., a Uyghur competence test) for the country's major minority languages also implies that these languages are *not* world-class languages and that Uyghur teachers and speakers do not have (nor have need of) high standards.

An unwritten (or covert) policy shift to a monocultural (monist) model for Xinjiang thus has shaped local cultural life in the last 20 years, from the rise of the artificial group term *Xinjiang ren* to the careful corralling off of the study of each Turkic language into its own academic department lest they gallop off together in a stampede of pan-Turkism. The PRC was consciously separating Turkic identities while conceptually joining newly-arrived Hans, Chinese-speaking Muslims, Mongols, Turkic speakers, and everyone else in Xinjiang into a new, constructed, unified identity. That new identity is entirely based in Chinese, as shown by the introduction of the HSK test and the lack of Uyghur competence on the part of Xinjiang Chinese.

> *An unwritten policy shift…has shaped local cultural life in the last 20 years*

Education

Overt Policies: Bilingual Education

Language instruction in Xinjiang is available at some schools in the following Category II & III languages: Uyghur, Kazak, Oyrat, Sibe, and Kyrgyz, as well as in Chinese. In December 1987, a joint commission of the Xinjiang Education Commission, the Minority Nationality Commission, and the Language Office formed an Autonomous Region minority primary- and middle-school working group charged with discussing how to implement bilingual education (Wang 1992: 248). As with so-called "bilingual education" in the United States, such policies were designed to help pupils make a rapid and smooth transition from their native language to the dominant language. In other words, instruction in the non-dominant language is limited to a transitional phase, until the pupil achieves dominant language competence. This bilingual education and teacher training promoted by the regional Party leadership and the Education Commission was designed to "swell the ranks of primary and secondary Chinese-language teachers, raise the quality of the Chinese-language teachers, improve the conditions of the Chinese-language teachers, and raise the status and treatment of Chinese-language teachers" (id.). Chinese-language curricular materials, first introduced in Xinjiang in the 1950s, underwent a major revision in 1985, including the development of 10 new textbooks for the added required elementary years (grades 3–6). The set of junior-college textbooks *Basic Chinese [Jichu Hanyu]*, originally published in 1955 and still used in tertiary institutions, also underwent five revisions by 1980. Moreover, Xinjiang Normal College produced six teacher-training volumes in 1988 (id: 249).

Covert Policies: Monolingualism through Educational Reform

Scholastic publishing
The consistent and heavy emphasis on writing—orthographic and lexical standardization—of PRC language policy has dwarfed other important language planning concerns, particularly the work to expand language-use domains in education. Neither the Language and Script Committee nor language researchers have directed their attention towards improving the quality of minority-language instruction and instructional materials.

However, Article 37 of the *Law of the People's Republic of China on Regional National Autonomy* (adopted May 1984 and amended February 2001) states that

> schools (classes and grades) and other institutions of education where most of the students come from minority nationalities shall, whenever possible, *use textbooks in their own languages, and use their languages as the media of instruction...* [emphasis added]. People's governments at various levels shall give financial support to the compilation, translation, and publishing of teaching materials and publications in languages of minority nationalities.[48]

Though basic textbooks did appear in the five policy-relevant languages of Xinjiang (Uyghur, Kazakh, Kyrgyz, Oyrat, and Sibe), only language-study textbooks were offered for the latter three languages. For other subject areas, pupils who spoke these languages were dependent on textbooks in Uyghur or Chinese. For Xinjiang's two largest minority groups, the Uyghurs and Kazakhs, scholastic publishing in the language was also often limited to the humanities and social sciences. Though some of these materials were created in the local language with some local illustrations (e.g., a Kazakh alphabet book or a Uyghur book of classical poetry), many other texts were not written in the local language. Gunnar Jarring reports that, in Kashgar in 1978, "Uyghur schoolbooks...were translated from Chinese and mostly printed in Peking" (Jarring 1986: 158).

No doubt both the frequent script changes and the political upheavals of the early PRC period hindered the development of pedagogical materials written directly in local languages. Not only did textbooks theoretically have to be reprinted every time there was a script change, but for over a decade during the Cultural Revolution, minority languages were not taught at all. For example, Uyghur was not taught in Kashgar (Jarring 1986: 157).

Languages of instruction

Many language policy issues concern the languages of instruction. Developing full competence in the Chinese language was and is seen as key to economic and social development. The level of Chinese competence in Xinjiang in the mid-1980s was markedly lower than in other minority areas of China—a shortfall, educators felt, attributable in equal parts to a lack of exposure to everyday Chinese and a lack of trained teachers. Both problems were more acute in impoverished rural southern Xinjiang than in the relatively more affluent north (Wang 1992).

But as policy in the mid-1980s seemed to be moving towards implementing the ideals of egalitarianism enshrined in the Constitution, including allowing unprecedented freedom of religious and cultural expression, 1984 was a watershed year for language policy in Xinjiang. The Autonomous Region Communist Party voted to expand the Chinese-language curriculum at all levels of education. Previously, non-Han pupils began formal study of Chinese in the first year of middle school; in 1984, that start was pushed back into primary school, so that children began learning Chinese formally in the third grade (Wang 1992: id.). The three extra primary years were coupled with an additional two intensive years of mandatory Chinese study at secondary and tertiary institutions—in effect, doubling formal instruction for non-Han students. Today, Chinese instruction in Xinjiang begins in the first grade.

As Naran Bilik indicates, the official promotion of Chinese stems from the assumption that Uyghur is not as useful as Chinese (the latter being a "quality" language). Uyghur is seen as

Today, Chinese instruction in Xinjiang begins in the first grade

backward. The central government's push to "Develop the West" should begin, in the view of one official in the Xinjiang Chinese standardized-testing HSK office, "with a change in the language of instruction" (Bilik n.d.). Furthermore, during an interview on the western channel of the Chinese Central Television (CCTV), "the CPC [Party] secretary of the Xinjiang UAR, Wang Lequan, state[d] that minority languages in Xinjiang contain only limited amounts of information, and cannot express some more advanced knowledge" (id.). This assertion is simply untrue: all languages, given proper language planning, are capable of complex expression.

Implementing Monolingualism in Education

Recent national education reform has moved toward decentralizing educational authority away from the national Education Commission and towards a two-tiered system in which local education commissions play a greater role (Duan 2003). While this shift may be a boon to the affluent areas of eastern China, it implies that local educational policies will be increasingly subject to local ideologies and economic resources. In Ürümchi, language policies focus on Chinese-only instruction.

The myth of school choice

The trend in Xinjiang towards monolingual education in the Han Chinese language can be seen at all levels of instruction. Since the 1980s, from preschool through secondary school, most urban parents had a choice between sending their children to a "Chinese [language]" school (or classroom, in the case of preschools) and a "nationality" (i.e., Uyghur-language) school. Non-Uyghur families (e.g., Han or Kazakh) invariably chose the national standard language over the regional lingua franca, and enrolled their children in the Han classrooms.

Uyghur families faced a more difficult choice. By choosing Uyghur schools, Uyghur parents hoped to sustain their children's ethnic identity by learning to read and write well in Uyghur. But enrolling their children in Han classrooms ensured that their children would have a higher competence in Chinese and better integration into Han society; whether or not this resulted in greater employment success is an urgent empirical research question. Observers report that those minority students with a Chinese-language education[49] tend to speak, dress, and act like Chinese students, which was both a source of prestige (vis-à-vis Han society) and embarrassment (vis-à-vis local ethnic identity, especially when their Uyghur skills slipped):

> The schools were widely recognized as the greatest integrating force, and the overwhelming conversion of Uyghur children to Han culture was resented. In cities where there was greater population of Uyghurs, they were far less likely to send their children to a Han school, but in Urumchi, it reached perhaps fifty percent (Light 1998).

A chronic lack of pedagogical materials was exacerbated by an apparent lack of economic resources. A symptomatic example is the allocation of material resources in the Xinjiang University preschool circa 1991: compared to the Chinese-language classrooms, "minority" (i.e., Uyghur) classrooms received half as many supplies and toys and even smaller pieces of drawing paper.[50]

School consolidation

In March 2004, the *Xinjiang Daily* announced that ethnic minorities in the region should now all have instruction in Chinese:

> The Chinese Communist Party and regional government have decided that ethnic minority schools must be merged with ethnic Chinese schools and ethnic minority students must be mixed with ethnic Chinese students. Teaching should be conducted in Chinese language as much as possible.... Some small towns and counties, where conditions are ripe, must start teaching Chinese to first-grade ethnic minority students in primary school (*Radio Free Asia* 2004).

The paper added that schools in Xinjiang currently employed Uyghur, Chinese, Kazakh, Kyrgyz, Mongol, Xibe [Sibe], and Russian, and that "this led to inefficiencies in the education system."

Since 1984, the Xinjiang Education Commission has gradually reduced Uyghur-language instruction at all levels. Until the mid-1990s, Chinese had been taught only as a second language in minority-language schools, *not* as a language of instruction. (All subjects except for the Chinese language were taught in the relevant minority language.) After the mid-1990s, however, Chinese became the language of instruction from third grade. Today, instruction in Chinese is required beginning in the first grade, and it is the minority language (e.g., Uyghur) that is taught as if it were a second language. Even preschools have reduced their minority-language (Uyghur) classrooms. At Xinjiang University, the number of minority-language classrooms was reduced during the 1990s from three to one and finally to zero.

Since the changes in the language of instruction, the differences between "minority-language schools" and "Chinese-language schools" became blurred. Therefore, beginning in the mid-1990s, the Education Commission started to merge these schools. In 2004, 50 Chinese and "minority" schools were consolidated in Xinjiang. While done in the name of efficiency, such school mergers are perceived as linguicide—the forced extinction of minority languages.

In contrast, Xinjiang's Central Asian neighbors have demonstrated that minority languages can be the language of instruction in schools without destabilizing the state (nor without any apparent detriment to the dominant language). In Kazakhstan, for example, schools educate about 30,000 Uyghur children in their native language; of these, 30 are exclusively Uyghur-language schools, and 30 are consolidated Russian-Uyghur-Kazakh schools. The government also sponsors a Uyghur-language theater and dance company (Working 2001; Nabijan Tursun March 2, 2004, pers. comm.). In Kyrgyzstan, a small number of schools offer Uyghur instruction, but only in three subjects (language, literature, and history), a narrow selection that is a point of contention for the local Uyghur population. Since 1994, however, the national State University has a faculty for Uyghur Philology (*Slovo Kyrgyzstana* 1998). Although Xinjiang's Uyghur population of about 8 million is much larger than those of its neighbors, there is no evidence that a Chinese government-controlled Uyghur-language school would foster separatism. On the contrary, allowing children to attend school in their native language would help dispel the impression now held by many Uyghurs that the government is systematically exterminating their language.

Ending Uyghur-language instruction
The final step of a long-term trend towards monolingualism occurred in May 2002, when it was decided that Xinjiang University would no

longer offer courses in the Uyghur language, at least in the first two years of coursework. This change was implemented in September 2002 (Große 2002).

Xinjiang University was founded in 1949 as a bilingual institution. Uyghur students were required to spend an extra first year at the university intensively studying Chinese, for a total of five university years. Although Han students only attended for four years, Uyghur language classes were part of the curriculum. For Uyghurs, most all of the curriculum was offered in the Uyghur language, including social sciences, natural sciences, and mathematics. Now, even Uyghur poetry is taught entirely in Chinese; only for Chagatay (Middle Turkic) poetry is the use of Uyghur in the classroom allowed.

According to the dean of Xinjiang University, this shift to university teaching in Chinese was crucial given the written and spoken "language deficits" in Uyghur students, which "often resulted in their falling behind their Han Chinese classmates" (Große 2002). The dean also cited the continued lack of adequate Uyghur-language course materials, particularly in the natural sciences. These arguments are circular: In essence, teaching in Chinese is necessary because Chinese was and is still being heavily promoted as the dominant language. Uyghur-language curricular deficits are directly related to the lack of political will, funding, and language codification necessary to commission, publish, and disseminate Uyghur-language materials. Finally, the lack of job prospects for Uyghur-track students was cited by the Xinjiang University dean as the most compelling reason for students to learn exclusively in Chinese (Große 2002).

After the 2002 declaration of monolingual university teaching, the HSK test was then pressed into service in Xinjiang to assess Chinese-language competence in minority teachers. Since 2002, 140 teachers whose Chinese was deemed inadequate for university pedagogy were forced into early retirement. Younger teachers without adequate standard Chinese language skills were asked to learn those skills by May 2004 or risk losing their jobs (Radio Free Asia 2004). Thus, all university educators in Xinjiang are now required to have a high degree of competence in Mandarin Chinese.[51]

Minority-language education in Xinjiang thus exemplifies the policy reversals described above. Until the mid-1980s, parents could choose native-language instruction for their children (albeit as part of bilingual education), and a number of pedagogical materials became available for the major minority languages such as Uyghur. But beginning in the late

1980s, cultural autonomy was progressively restricted: Chinese language instruction was expanded, minority-language instruction was curtailed, and minority and Chinese schools were consolidated.

Beijing saw these changes as an economic necessity, meant to stem minority unemployment in Xinjiang through ensuring all teachers and pupils would have a high competence in Chinese. Minorities in Xinjiang—particularly Uyghurs—have perceived the changes to monolingual instruction as a cultural attack; and this perception has fostered the very identity polarization (Uyghur versus Chinese) that Beijing would like to neutralize.

> *Uyghurs...perceive the change to monolingual instruction as a cultural attack*

Identity, of course, is multilayered, and need not be diametric; it is entirely possible to have a strong Uyghur identity and simultaneously be a citizen of China. Additionally, many Xinjiang denizens identify themselves as part of the Central Asian cultural sphere.

The Role of English

Policies on the languages of instruction in China's minority regions are now beginning to be driven by forces other than the government's education commissions; namely, by market forces and the media. On China's eastern seaboard, both market demand (particularly in service and export industries) and media presence have prompted a boom in English language pedagogy. Uyghur pupils, students, and their parents are also starting to demand more and better-quality English instruction. In the PRC, English "is considered one of the three basic subjects in school the other two being *yuwen* [i.e., Chinese] and mathematics" (Li 2000: 85).

English as an International Language
Hegemonic though it may be, English is one path towards economic development and internationalization. Many analysts today consider India to have an economic advantage over China precisely because of the high rate of English fluency among educated Indian citizens. By contrast, China has for years specialized in a non-conversational rote-learning of English, what is affectionately known to university students as *yaba yingyu* ("mute English"). China has recognized the importance of English: For example, CCTV-9 is exclusively broadcasting in English, and Shanghai TV has bilingual Mandarin-English programming.

International trade, which often requires a variety of English-language skills, has flourished under selective state incentives, including the creation of Special Economic Zones (one of which—Khorgas—is located in Xinjiang). Besides its role in international communication, English is seen as a vehicle to economic and social mobility (Zhao and Campbell 1995). Nonetheless, some observers argue that incentives to learn foreign languages like English are not yet great enough and the costs too high to warrant their mandatory instruction at all levels of education (McKay, in Gray 2003). English instruction, however, is one important method of advancement and employment for Uyghurs.

Learning English in Xinjiang
New techniques of English teaching are so far confined to China's prosperous east coast. Since the 1980s, the monolingual English four-volume textbook series *New Concept English* and its bilingual Chinese-English translation *Xin gainian Yingyu* have been available throughout China (Alexander 1967; Anonymous 2002a). When English is taught to minorities, it is taught through the medium of Chinese; 80 percent of Uyghurs learn English through Chinese. The remainder learns more or less directly from English. In Xinjiang, however, authorities justify the lack of Uyghur-language English textbooks by stating that there is no demand for such instruction, so that Chinese textbooks can be used.

English is taught to minorities...through the medium of Chinese

There are a number of reasons why minorities, especially the Uyghurs, should learn English directly, either via a monolingual English textbook or a bilingual Uyghur-English textbook. On the issue of monolingual versus bilingual textbooks, the Chinese experience is instructive: English classes at Chinese universities are generally of far less quality than those taught by private tutors (either individually or at schools). With a tutor, English is often taught directly through near-monolingual instruction in English, whereas at universities, not only is English taught *through* Chinese, but also nearly monolingually *in* Chinese, with occasional rote recitation in English. Although there are notable exceptions in some classrooms, universities tend to teach by rote rather than by analytic thinking. Yet there are now no alternatives to university English classes: Across Xinjiang, private English instruction was shut down by the PRC government in the mid-1990s, amid concerns that private schools could be conduits for anti-government political propaganda.

A further argument for the direct learning of English concerns language structure. Uyghur's vocabulary contains a number of Indo-European lexemes, loan words from Russian and Persian. While Chinese is a tone-based language, both English and Uyghur are stress-based. In addition, Uyghur has a larger consonant and vowel inventory than does Chinese, making most English sounds easier for Uyghur speakers to learn. For all these reasons, by the accident of language typology, combined with the common Indo-European vocabulary, speakers of Uyghur are on average able to learn English much more rapidly and with more accurate pronunciation than their Chinese-speaking counterparts. (Japanese, which after English is the most commonly studied language in China, is even easier for Uyghurs to learn.) Teaching English directly via Uyghur will require textbooks and an English-Uyghur dictionary.[52]

For Uyghurs, learning English through the medium of Chinese is not just irritating; it also guarantees that these students will forever be playing catch-up to their Han Chinese counterparts. An English word such as *computer* must first be learned through the Chinese gloss *diannao*, instead of via the perfectly good Uyghur word (of Russian origin) *kompyuter*.

By having to study English through the medium of Chinese, Uyghurs are prone to fall behind native Chinese-speaking students in school. The results of such a policy-induced learning handicap can easily be misinterpreted by policymakers and the general public as evidence that Uyghur is a "low quality" language.

Language Sequencing

The current trend towards monolingualism in Xinjiang is repeatedly justified by the supposed economic benefits of speaking and writing Chinese. But would using Uyghur and other non-Han languages hinder the advancement of Xinjiang's minorities? It shouldn't. Many other countries promote the use of three or more languages. South Africa, for example, is a country with eleven official languages and a language policy that aims to ensure equality for all language groups. In India, which has a three-language policy, each region of the country promotes its major regional language, Hindi, and English. Countries such as South Africa and India thus officially resist the hegemony of any one language (particularly English); English is simply learned as an additional language, as it is in Scandinavia.

Other experiences with the sequencing of dominant and non-dominant languages are relevant for China. Current Ethiopian policy suggests one such avenue. Ethiopia is a country with theoretically nineteen languages of instruction in primary schools. However, in practice, only the dominant languages are supported. As with China, Ethiopia has a dominant language, Amharic, major minority languages (Oromo and Tigrinya), and over 100 other languages. Since 1991, Ethiopia's ethnoregional policy has introduced languages in sequences into schools, based on the dominant regional language. In Tigrinya-speaking areas, for instance, the language of instruction is Tigrinya; English is introduced from the first grade, and Amharic is introduced in the third grade. Though the implementation of this policy nationwide has not been problem-free for Ethiopia, China, with a per capita GDP seven times that of Ethiopia and hence with considerably more resources available for language support, could easily implement similar language sequences. Ideally, in minority areas, parents would have a choice of sequences (Chinese-track or major minority language-track), both including English. The child's native or best language would be the first and only language of instruction until grade 3, when the national language, Chinese, would be introduced. English would be taught from grade 5 on. A similar tracking system has been suggested for eastern China as the best use of educational and economic resources.[53]

English instruction in Xinjiang reflects the weaker implementation of newer foreign-language education policy initiatives in minority areas. By improving both the availability of English instruction and teaching methodology as well as by reinstating educational opportunities in major minority languages, the PRC government has an opportunity to gain goodwill among its minority citizens. A second critical area for such interventions is minority-language media.

Media: Official Representations of Xinjiang and the Uyghurs

The 1984 Law on Regional Autonomy encouraged the dissemination of literature, print and broadcasting news, films, and television in the languages of the titular minority Autonomous Regions. It called for the collection and publication of their books and the preservation of their historical and cultural heritage. Unlike educational policy, media law (at least for print publications) has been and continues to be implemented nearly to the letter, albeit with a rigorous political screening process.

Print Publications

Since the 1980s, publishing houses have been the beneficiaries of government support for the widespread dissemination of Uyghur literature.[54] Not only did edited volumes of various literary genres become available (such as prose poems, ballads, and humorous stories), but also a number of quasi-academic journals were launched during this period. These included the literary journals *Tarim*; *Bulaq* (1981–present); and the linguistics journal *Language and Translation* (*Til wä Tärjimä/Yuyan yu fanyi*). The latter is published in Chinese, Uyghur, Kazakh, and Oyrat Mongolian editions.

The selection of titles published in a given language is generally proportionate to the size and stature of the group (see the ethnolinguistic hierarchy in Figure 1). Thus, Chinese-language publications are the most numerous, with local, regional, and national daily newspapers and academic journals. Uyghur-language publications are plentiful but somewhat less numerous; there are half as many Kazakh publications, and only a smattering of those in Kyrgyz. Other ethnic groups do not, as a rule, enjoy print media.[55]

Unlike other areas of media and education, non-scholastic print publications do a good job of supporting minority-language maintenance in China. Available offerings are, relatively speaking, topically diverse, addressed to a wide range of reader ages, and widely distributed. Most recent book-length publications are being written directly in the relevant minority language, unlike news media.

Non-Scholastic Publishing

The 1980s heralded a brief period of effort to create a multilingual society, although it was Chinese-dominant and by no means represented an equal division of linguistic resources.

While Chinese remained the default language, more major minority-language media and educational resources were available than ever before. Publishing houses expanded their offerings dramatically. Previously, titles had tended to be practical (e.g., agricultural manuals); academic (schoolbooks and dictionaries); or political (e.g., an official history of Xinjiang). Many of these works were translated directly from Chinese, with no attempt to adapt the contents to the local context. Beginning in the early 1980s, non-scholastic books in Uyghur for children began to appear, as well as dubbed Chinese and local Uyghur television broadcasts.

Compared to many other language domains, publishing in major minority languages is much more in line with China's overt policy of fostering all its official languages. By 1998, over 4,100 book titles in 23 minority languages had been published in China (Information Office...1999b); in Xinjiang, more than 100 titles have been published (Xinhua 2003). Compared to the near total lack of materials published in Xinjiang in the early to mid-20th century, where printing basically began with the Swedish mission in Kashgar,[56] this abundance of publications is indeed a very impressive accomplishment.

The 1984 *Law on Regional Autonomy* emphasized both minority-language materials and the rendering of these materials into Chinese: "The organs of self-government of national autonomous areas shall...*translate* and publish historical and cultural books of minority nationalities...so as to inherit and develop their outstanding traditional culture" (Zhongguo...zizhifa 2001; emphasis added). State support of minority-language publications is laudable. But the emphasis on translation as a means of cultural development recalls the "minority quality" argument, implying that minority texts can only be understood by removing them from their linguistic contexts and rendering them in the dominant "quality" language.

The 1980s and 1990s saw Chinese policy moving in opposite directions: While policy towards multiple forms of cultural expression was liberalizing rapidly, education policy steered away from pluralism and towards monoculturalism.

Minority-language publishing in Xinjiang

The early days of the PRC heralded, as the *Law* stipulates, translations of "quality culture" in the form of major Chinese historical novels such as a Uyghur-language *Hong Lou Meng* ("Dream of the Red Chamber"), a Sibe-language version of *Xi you ji* ("Journey to the West"), and Mongolian translations of *Sanguo yanyi* ("Romance of the Three Kingdoms") and *Jin gu qi guan* ("Grotesque Tales Present and Past"). Unlike translations into other languages, the vast majority of those works ultimately rendered in Mongolian and Sibe were re-translated via Manchu from Chinese (Jagchid and Hyer 1979: 219).

In the 1980s, a number of philological, literary, and textual works important to Uyghur culture were reprinted or published for the first time. Three major representative publications were (1) a modern Uyghur translation of 11th century Turkic dictionary, the *Divan lugat at-türk*, compiled by Mahmud al-Kashgari; (2) another work written in Kashgar, Yusuf Khass Hajip's *Qutadghu bilik* ("The Wisdom of Royal Glory"); and (3) a textual exegesis of the 9th century Buddhist manuscript *Maytri simit* ("Encounters with Maitreya").[57] Taken together, such works define the rich Uyghur historical and cultural heritage: Turkic (as distinct from Arab and Persian); Buddhist; and Muslim. In conjunction with the relaxation of restrictions on religious freedom, in 1987 a Uyghur-language rendering of the *Qur'an* was published.

Major works in other languages were published locally in Xinjiang as well during the 1980s, e.g., a two-volume account in Oyrat of the legendary hero *Jangger khan* (Xinjiang Renmin, 1987) and a version of *Geser khan* (a heroic epic of Tibetan origin, Xinjiang Renmin, 1989). These works served to define Oyrat historical identity, much as *Qutadghu Bilik* and other works do for the Uyghurs. These days, there is even a publicly sponsored Uyghur literary website.[58]

Publishers have also done a fine job of bringing out a number of important language reference works. Beginning in 1979 with the Latin-script Uyghur-Chinese dictionary (published and then reissued in 1982 by Xinjiang University), several useful bilingual dictionaries have appeared, and a major six-volume monolingual encyclopedia on Uyghur with 60,000 entries was later compiled (Yakub et al. 1990–99). In addition, a few reference works on other languages have been published. Such works are primarily in the second-largest language of Xinjiang, Kazakh, and include dictionaries (Chinese-Kazakh in Latin script in 1979, and Kazakh-Chinese in Arabic-based script in 1989); grammars; and a multi-volume encyclopedia (which was actually a Russian encyclopedia re-issued in the Arabic Kazakh script).

Uyghur literary journals had already begun to appear in the late 1970s and early 1980s: first *Bulaq* ("Wellspring") and *Kashgar ädäbiyat sän'iti* ("Kashgar Literature and Art"), and later *Tarim, Dunya Ädibiyati* ("World Literature") appeared. These journals, which are still issued today, contain poems, short stories, and editorials. Most tertiary institutions (such as Xinjiang University, Xinjiang Institute of Technology, and Kashgar Teacher's College) have their own journals in Chinese, yet most of these journals do not have Uyghur editions. Some scholarly journals are published in minority languages: Xinjiang Kyrgyz Literature (1981–present); Xinjiang Gazetteer (*Shinjang täzkirichiliki*, 1983–present); and the Kazakh literary journal *Mura*. The Oyrats do not have a monthly academic journal except for the Oyrat edition of *Language and Translation*; a Chakhar Mongolian language journal, *Mongol xel bichig*, is published in Hohhot.

The relative abundance of literary works and scholarly journals in the major minority languages of Xinjiang stemmed from the multilingual policy of the 1980s. These works continue to be published well after the shift to a monolingual policy in the 1990s, a shift that primarily affected the domains of education and the broadcast media.

Newspapers, Broadcasting, and Film

Language policy for the media has caused a decline in the number of Uyghur language domains. Since the 1980s, the media space devoted to Chinese and the pace of sinicization of Uyghur vocabulary have increased. The systematic replacement of many words of Russian origin by Chinese (such as *dianhua* for *telefon*, "telephone") is the direct result of language policies for news media.

> *Language policy...has caused a decline in the number of Uyghur language domains*

The American website of the PRC embassy proclaims that "[t]he number of newspapers increased from 4 in 1952 to 98 in 2001, of which 43 were published in local ethnic-minority languages" (Embassy of the PRC in the USA 2003). By official count, about 100 newspapers in 17 minority languages and 73 periodicals in 11 minority languages are published in China today. But of the daily newspapers in Uyghur and Kazakh (such as the *Xinjiang Daily* and the *People's Daily*), all but the most local editions are translated from the Chinese editions of these newspapers. These quick and often literal translations promulgate a kind of Uyghur "governmentese" that can be far removed from modern standard Uyghur. In particular, these dailies promote the substitution of Chinese terms for existing Uyghur lexemes, for example, *palü* (from Chinese *falü*) instead of *qanun* ("law").

Television and radio broadcasts in foreign languages are increasingly available, particularly in eastern China. But broadcasting in minority languages reached its peak in the early 1990s and has been progressively reduced ever since. Of the 43 national television stations, seven were broadcasting as of 2002 in one or more languages in addition to Mandarin Chinese: foreign language programming on Shanghai TV in English; and on CCTV 1–9 in English, French, Japanese, Russian, and German. The national broadcasters in Inner Asia vary greatly in the frequency of their minority-language offerings. Inner Mongolia TV does not broadcast in

Mongolian; Tibet TV (a private company) and Qinghai TV broadcast in Tibetan and Mandarin; and Xinjiang TV broadcasts in Uyghur, Kazakh, and Mandarin (Anon. 2002b). But beginning in 1999, Xinjiang TV and Xinjiang [radio] Broadcasting reduced their full Uyghur-language broadcasts to multilingual ones, with a maximum of eight hours of Uyghur per day. Broadcast media in the more minor languages (Category III and lower) were also reduced.

There are local TV stations that broadcast some of their programming in local languages; however, most broadcast in Mandarin only (e.g., in Xinjiang, Xinjiang Economic TV, Ürümchi TV, Karamay TV, and others). Radio broadcasting has been slightly more multilingual: Nationwide, 20 minority languages enjoyed at least brief airtime by stations at the national, prefectural, or regional level. The Central People's Broadcasting radio network (transmitted throughout China) has offered some programming in sixteen languages (Information Office 1999b).

Cinema and television films are legally required to be made in the Chinese language. If a film is designated for a minority-area viewership, then it will be dubbed into the relevant local language. This means that Uyghur actors in a drama on Uyghur culture made at the Xinjiang Film Studio must say their lines in Chinese, and then have a Uyghur soundtrack dubbed over the Chinese. A *People's Daily* White Paper states that 10,430 films have been dubbed in minority languages (Information Office 1999b). News broadcasts are also produced in Chinese and then translated into the major local language. Foreign films and television series are dubbed both in standard Chinese and sometimes the local languages; popular fare in the 1990s included the German detective series *Derrick* and the American series *Dallas* (dubbed in Uyghur), and *Donald Duck* dubbed in Kazakh. This cumbersome translation process, while ensuring political control of content, has accelerated the sinicization of minority-language vocabulary.

There is thus a dichotomy in the implementation of Chinese media policy in Xinjiang. While both minority-language print and broadcast media have appeared in volume since the mid-1980s, only the print media can be said to be growing in volume. Each year, new Uyghur (and to a far lesser extent, Kazakh, Kyrgyz, and Sibe) print publications appear in a variety of genres. Given that at least half of all films, videos, and radio broadcasts intended for minority-language audiences are produced in Chinese "translatese," the net effect has been to undermine major minority languages. Though the "translatese" may well be attributable primarily to the severe time constraints of translation, the practice often sparks unnecessary resentment in the minority-language community.

While the implementation of media policy in Xinjiang as discussed above is purely a domestic and a regional issue, discourse *about* Xinjiang has become an international issue. In the next section, we turn to media policy for national and international discourse about Xinjiang, the Uyghurs, and Uyghur nationalism.

Covert Language Policy: The Politicization of Discourse

Connotation Management

Worldwide, government planners, national and international media, and members of ethnolinguistics groups all negotiate *de facto* covert language policy as part of a broader negotiation of ethnic identity. While all languages of China under overt, *de jure* policy are theoretically equal, *de facto* policies promote an unequal division of power and resources (both linguistic and material) among different ethnolinguistic groups. The media and governmental bodies play an important role in shaping public perceptions about the legitimacy and standing of languages and in the distribution of resources. This constitutes the *implementation* of covert policy.

de facto policies promote an unequal division of power and resources

Language policy crucially involves not only codifying words themselves, but also codifying their use. This has been accomplished through the repetition of key words or phrases in the public discourse. These collocations are laden with political content. Such connotation management is characteristic of political discourse everywhere. What makes the Chinese case interesting is the PRC's use of ethnoreligious and geographical nomenclature in the international context to gird one specific group, the Uyghurs, to the concept of the modern Chinese nation. The dissemination of specific collocations, including the ones cited below, is more than a simple choice of vocabulary. Instead, these collocations represent often bitter negotiations over what constitutes Uyghur cultural and linguistic heritage.

Language Policing

Throughout the history of the People's Republic, a political committee has censored media in any language. In Xinjiang, before publication, all articles in all languages have had to be vetted by a publications committee (known as *Näshiriyat mätbär täkshürüp bekitisi orun*). Since 1998 and particularly since 2000, as the Uyghur language is phased out of tertiary institutions, newer forms of language policing have taken shape. Even classes on Uyghur literature and poetry, now taught entirely in Chinese, are subject to spot checks by people referred to informally as language police (*til saqchi*).

Chinese versus Local-Language Nomenclature
The official use of sinicized toponyms in minority areas (e.g., *Tacheng* for *Chöchäk*, *Kashi* for *Kashgar*) reinforces the impression that minority languages are being deliberately eradicated, although such toponyms are simply an aspect of a unified national policy rendering all official nomenclature in Mandarin.[59] Language planning efforts to reverse at least the trend towards lexical replacement would lessen the perception that local languages are threatened; since language is central to identity, such simple measures might remove fuel from the potential fires of separatism.

"Xinjiang" versus "Eastern Turkestan"
The geographic term *Western Regions*, connotes far more than simply the "regions to the west;" it is simultaneously imbued with the ancient Han view of China's territories and the modern Chinese development of its backward border regions. A similarly laden toponym is *Eastern Turkestan* (or *Turkistan*). Originally, it was simply a Persian geographic term meaning "land of the Turks." Beginning in the 19th century, *Eastern Turkestan* was employed both by Turkic nationalists (Aubin 1998) and by Russians to distinguish the Tarim and Junggarian Basins from Western Turkestan, which refers to the regions west of the Pamir Mountains. At present, however, the pan-Turkic sentiment imbued in the term *Eastern Turkestan*—the "eastern homeland of the Turks"—is in the view of PRC authorities antithetical to national unity; the term has thus been declared illegal in China.[60]

In the last 40 years, and particularly since 1990, disgruntled Uyghurs have nonetheless revived *Eastern Turkestan* as a nationalist designation. Though the term is often assumed to imply political separatism, it does not necessarily do so. Some Uyghurs and their supporters, particularly those with separatist sympathies, view the designation *Eastern Turkestan* with primordialist eyes. ("It is

disgruntled Uyghurs have...revived Eastern Turkestan as a nationalist designation

the best term to represent our homeland," said one.) Other Uyghurs use it to signal a strong ethnic identity in the face of Han socioeconomic dominance, preferring *Eastern Turkestan* to *Xinjiang* ("new dominion"), given the latter's ponderously colonialist tone.

Ironically, however, despite being banned for ordinary citizens, *Eastern Turkestan* is now lavishly used in one context: in government reports on "terrorism" within China. These largely undocumentable condemnations, which are routinely republished by Western news media and governments, detail over 50 "Eastern Turkestan separatist groups" several of whose very existence is in question.

A cursory survey of Chinese- and English-language websites for the term *Eastern Turkestan* reveals a steady increase in its use in both languages on all websites, to over 6,000 sites for the first three quarters of 2004 alone. Comparing the ratio of PRC sites to all sites using the term, I observe that the English-language term *Eastern Turkestan* occurred most frequently on PRC sites associated with the year 2001 (19 percent of all sites); the equivalent Chinese-language term *Dong Tujuesitan* peaked in 2000 and 2001 (96 percent and 91 percent, respectively). Since the term is officially banned, its high-frequency use on PRC websites suggests the term is being used for propaganda purposes. *Eastern Turkestan* is used on many of these pages in association with highly negative political terms such as *splittist*, *separatist*, and *terrorist*, leading readers to associate the place name with danger and chaos. This reappropriation is the essence of connotation management: A geographic label that had been once co-opted by overseas Uyghur nationalist groups agitating for autonomy or independence has been co-opted again by the Chinese government media as a means of counteracting Uyghur nationalism.

Figure 2. Google™ Search Results for "Eastern Turkestan" (Sept. 27, 2004)

Term	*Dong Tujuesitan***		*Eastern Turkestan****	
lang.	Chinese	Chinese	English	English
Domain / year*	on all web sites	on PRC sites alone (% of total)	on all web sites	on PRC sites alone (% of total)
1980	116	34 (29%)	955	60 (6%)
1990	1180	495 (42%)	1378	176 (13%)
2000	796	761 **(96%)**	4220	306 (7%)
2001	996	903 **(91%)**	4000	793 **(19%)**
2002	1660	1250 (75%)	4280	369 (9%)
2003	1950	1340 (69%)	3930	610 (15%)
2004	**1670**	771 (46%)	**4430**	408 (9%)

*Year was mentioned somewhere on the relevant web page; it is not necessarily the year the page was produced.
**In Chinese characters
***Including variant spellings *Turkestan/Turkistan*

Even though such a preliminary search oversimplifies the data,[61] that the percentage of PRC-site hits has decreased overall since 2003 indicates that both *Dong Tujuesitan* and "Eastern Turkestan" occur more frequently on Western websites, suggesting that the topic is now more salient for Western media, governments, NGOs, and discussion groups (including those of overseas Uyghurs).

The Public Discourse Shift

The PRC government attributed the isolated but repeated unrest in Xinjiang during the mid-1990s to China's liberalization of religious and linguistic policy in the region a decade earlier. Other possible reasons for the unrest (for example, that the liberalization policies did not go far enough, or that they crucially neglected to include political freedoms) appear to have been rejected.

unrest in Xinjiang... [was attributed] to China's liberalization of religious and linguistic policy

Even limited autonomy for the major national minorities, the government concluded, threatened the stability of the region. The result was a crackdown in Xinjiang known as the "Strike Hard" campaign. That 1996 campaign ushered in a new period of high profile police activity, but its associated rhetoric initially represented no change from previous policy. Nominally an anti-crime measure, "Strike Hard" also took steps against "political activists," including "pro-independence activists" (Pike 1999). But by late 2001, this nearly respectful rhetoric would be dispensed with.

The mid-1990s however saw a concomitant increase in the sophistication of PRC rhetoric used to describe Chinese-minority relations. For the first time, in addition to a domestic media discourse in standard Chinese on these relations, a distinct international discourse targeted at English speakers also emerged. Domestic rhetoric from this period emphasized the "one big family" concept of ethnic relations (*yi jiazu*, "one family")[62] as well as the slightly dated-sounding but still current *xiongdi minzu* ("fraternal nationalities,"—literally, "older brother-younger brother nationalities"). In contrast, political rhetoric in English (in newspapers and on websites) alludes to a profoundly pluralistic and egalitarian policy by using terms such as "multicultural society" and "multiethnic society" to describe China's relations with its minorities. The Chinese domestic rhetoric thus still includes a noticeable element of condescension towards minority nationalities, a condescension that is absent in discourse directed towards an international audience. If the trends in discourse on minorities in Taiwan—where an earlier condescending term *shanbao* ("mountain brothers") was replaced by *yuanjumin* ("aboriginal peoples")—provide an instructive parallel, then we can expect the PRC domestic discourse on minorities to become more respectful in coming years.

The 1996 Shift to "Uyghur Separatists"
The official Chinese discourse associated with political events thus has become a weathervane for changes in cultural policy, including for language. Since the 1950s, Xinjiang security forces have been tracking "splittists," who have been termed the greatest threat to the nation. An example of this early rhetoric on "splittists"—the official research study on "Pan-Islamism and Pan-Turkism" (Xinjiang Acad. Soc. Sci. 1994)—cited what it termed "incidents of ethnic rebellion" which occurred in the XUAR from the 1950s to the early 1990s. The book attacked nationalist intellectuals in Xinjiang for generating "counter-revolutionary *separatist thinking* among the public" through their literary works and scholarly research.

After the 1997 riots in Ghulja (Yining), the demonstrators arrested were charged with "splittism, counter-revolutionary and criminal activity, and fundamentalist religious activity"(id.). Though religious fundamentalism was one of the four charges, the "Strike Hard" campaign was primarily aimed at *separatists* ("splittists") rather than religious terrorists. Separatism was also seen overwhelmingly as a domestic issue rather than a transnational one. Then-President Jiang Zemin's use of language in 1998, for example, contains little mention of religion in conjunction with Xinjiang, and much concern over Uyghur nationalism. Jiang was quoted about Xinjiang: "The tree may prefer calm, but the wind will not subside. It will be a long-term task to fight *splittism*" (BBC 1998).[63]

A comparison of Jiang's 1998 statement with a January 2002 Chinese Foreign Ministry announcement on unrest in Xinjiang reveals how the rhetoric has shifted entirely away from domestic Uyghur nationalism ("splittism") and towards religious-based international terrorism: "These people have links with the Bin Laden clique and have been infected with the *jihad mentality*," the announcement read. "We should regard cracking down on these *terrorists* as part of the *international struggle* against terrorism" (Ash 2004, emphasis added).[64] Then, in December 2003, the PRC "released a statement identifying 'Uyghur *terrorist* organizations and leaders'" (id., emphasis added). The references to terrorism and global Islam are new.

Post-9/11: "Terrorists" in Service of Monoculturalism

Since August 2002, the ethnonym *Uyghur* has been associated with terrorism in the international and domestic press. At that time, the U.S. State Department listed the Eastern Turkestan Islamic Movement (ETIM)—apparently associated with a handful of Uyghurs—as a Foreign Terrorist Organization (FTO). This official listing appeared to equate Uyghurs both with terrorism and with radical Islam.[65]

> *the ethnonym Uyghur has been associated with terrorism*

Confusion between "separatism" and "terrorism"

In the international press since 2001, it has become customary to associate the ethnonym Uyghur with the religious terms *Islam* and *Muslim* (as in *the Muslim Uyghurs*).[66] This association also has become common in news headlines and bylines: "China targets terror in western majority Muslim region" (*Chicago Sun-Times*, 2004); "Some Uyghur activists in Muslim areas of western China are said to be affiliated with al-Qaeda" (Katzman 2002; Information Office 1999a). In the English-language press, Uyghurs are often confusingly referred to as "Chinese Muslims."[67] The weekly *Die Zeit* mentions "Uyghurs, the Islamic group" in the same sentence as "terrorists."[68]

With the complicity of much of the international press, China can claim the lion's share of responsibility for introducing and promulgating this discourse shift. Just a week after 9/11, the Foreign Ministry spokesman Zhu Bangzao stated: "China...has reasons to ask the United States to give its support and understanding in the fight against terrorism and separatists" (FlorCruz 2001).

In a 2002 interview conducted by and published in *Die Zeit*, Beijing University vice-president and biogenetics professor Chen Zhangliang and Chinese rock musician Cui Jian clearly equated Uyghurs with terrorists, although the interviewees attributed this position to the American and Chinese governments and to the UN (Blume 2002):

> *Die Zeit*: As for China's national cohesion, there is another problem: that of the Uyghurs in Xinjiang Province [sic]. Do you consider the Islamic rebels who live among the Uyghurs as dissidents or terrorists?

> *Cui*: The Chinese regime considers them terrorists without a doubt.

Chen: The United Nations and George W. Bush have confirmed this viewpoint.

International media reports also reveal that China escalated its rhetoric connecting Uyghurs, Islam, and terrorism. In 2002, separatist Uyghurs were described in one official account as being part of a "holy war":

> ...[t]he report also said that bin Laden and his network had provided money, weapons and other equipment to help Chinese terrorists "*launch a 'holy war' aimed at setting up a theocratic 'Islamic state' in Xinjiang*" (emphasis added). It provided no evidence, however, to support the claim" (Pan 2002).

Some journalists, recognizing that the conflict is primarily one of domestic separatism rather than international terrorism, identify the conflation of "separatist" and "terrorist" (Schmidt-Häuer 2001; Chung 2002; Kurlantzick 2004).

Discourse tailored for the West
What is notable about the discourse on terrorism is the difference in frequency of usage before and after September 11, 2001. Comparing online sources only, an Internet search (via Google™) in English and Chinese for the terms *Uyghur separatists* and *Uyghur terrorists* (and their variants) together with years yielded two significant findings (see Figure 3).

Figure 3: Search Results for "Separatists" versus "Terrorists" (June 13, 2004)

concept	Uyghur separatists		Uyghur terrorists	
language	English	Chinese	English	Chinese
term(s) / year	"Uyghur** separatists"****	"Weiwuer(zu) fenliezhuyizhe"****	"Uyghur terrorists" **	"Weiwuer(zu) kongbufenzi" ****
1980	128	0	6	0
1990	391	2	58	1
2000	867	5	209	6
2001	**1160**	**5**	208	**6**
2002	927	3	188	1
2003	801	2	**214**	0
2004	795	2	158	0

*Year was mentioned somewhere on the relevant web page; it is not necessarily the year that the page was produced.

**Including variant spellings *Uyghur/Uighur/Uygur*.

***Including the terms *separatist* and *splittist*.

****In Chinese characters, including the variants *Weiwuer/Weiwuerzu*.

First, the peak usage of each term differed by two years: While "separatists" peaked in 2001 (with 1,160 results), "terrorists" peaked in 2003 (with 214). Second, the English-language web pages with these collocations far outnumbered the Chinese pages.

The paucity of results for the Chinese-language search suggests that this discourse on terrorism is actually intended for an international audience, not a domestic one. Primary targets include the English-language media of China, Uyghur overseas activists, and non-Chinese policy makers and NGOs.

The difference in peak usage reflects the American and international need for discourse about "terrorism" after September 11, 2001. Chinese and other media stepped in to fill that need. Dovetailing neatly with Chinese cultural policy towards the Uyghurs, this recent media shift to rhetoric on Uyghur "terrorism" justifies the establishment of a Chinese monocultural area in Xinjiang.

The results of the search in Figure 2 on *Eastern Turkestan* were slightly different than for the terms *separatist* and *terrorist*. Use of the term *Eastern Turkestan* peaked in 2000 and 2001 on Chinese sites—i.e., before and during the September 11-inspired rhetorical shift.[69] Apparently *Eastern Turkestan* is more associated with the older rhetoric about *Uyghur separatists/splittists*, as is indicated in Figure 3 by the high frequency of these terms during the same period. During and after 2001, however, the shift towards a frequent use of "Uyghur terrorists" is unmistakable.

Western ignorance about the Uyghurs, Xinjiang, Chinese ethnic geopolitics, and even about "terrorism" have rendered the Western media an easy victim to the manipulation of discourse. Although China has been careful to focus on organizations and individuals, media rhetoric has lead Westerners into thinking that Uyghurs are dangerous. The Chinese state media has been making use of Western credulity to enhance China's control over a restive region.

state media...[used] Western credulity to enhance China's control over a restive region

Linguistic Nationalism and Transnational Issues

In contrast to Xinjiang, the Central Asian republics, which are also primarily Turkic-speaking, have shifted away from policies minimizing linguistic nationalism to those encouraging it, by "raising the status of the titular *ethnie* to state language, with certain provisions for Russian and all other languages spoken in the republic" (Landau and Kellner-Heinkele 2001). This support of linguistic nationalism west of the Pamirs has, in conjunction with the CCP's local response to international events, been one factor contributing to the monolingual trend in Xinjiang.

As implemented in Chinese Inner Asia, regional autonomy and a monoethnic state appear to be fundamentally contradictory. Chinese policies such as the Law on Regional National Autonomy were unenforceable. In the last 20 years, China has poured resources into infrastructural development and natural-resource exploitation in the Autonomous Regions, especially in the campaign to Develop the Western Regions. Meanwhile, the government has reduced resource allocation for indigenous language support in these regions, a move that has engendered enmity among the local populace. If the central government wants to win back the hearts and minds of some of its Xinjiang citizenry, it needs to devote material and human resources to fostering major local languages and to balancing the language needs of differently sized groups, just as Central Asia policymakers must balance the needs of Russians and other minorities. Yet the Chinese government's response to this dilemma has been to treat language support as though it were support of separatism. I suggest that CCP language and cultural support of minorities actually quell separatist tendencies. Having a separate ethnic identity does not necessarily entail anti-majority sentiment. While Turkic speakers of Inner Asia have long had a distinct identity, the pressure of China's monoculturalist policy has reframed the psychologically healthy ethnic sentiment of being distinct (that of being "different than Hans") into a politicized anti-majority feeling (being "anti-Han"). Economic disparities and the state's routine rhetorical dichotomies ("Han/minority," "Inner/Outer Mongolia," or "New/Old Orthography") have encouraged the major minorities to hold the Han Chinese in similar contempt. Implementing the constitutional ideals of the PRC, which direct that Uyghur and other minority languages be valued on the basis of their own cultures, would in contrast drastically reduce the tension in Xinjiang.

Chinese nationalism for a "unitary, multiethnic country" is at an all-time high, and aims to stave off perceived ideological threats from the outside. One such "threat" is the potentially Turkic monolingual language policies of the neighboring Central Asian republics. Yet even Turkic

China's monoculturalist policy has reframed the psychologically healthy ethnic sentiment

nationalists in the republics had to concede during the 1990s that Russian was too practical to abandon, just as Malaysia had to reluctantly move from its Malay-only language policy if that country were to develop and prosper in the international economy. If major minorities in Xinjiang regain the opportunity to study and support their languages, they will still want to learn and use Chinese, just as the Kyrgyz have continued to study Russian and the Malays have continued to study English.

Conflicts affect access to and maintenance of resources, including critical linguistic resources. Language is nearly always central to ethnic identity. A language is not a generic communication implement, but embodies nearly every dimension of a given culture in a unique way: ritual and routine activity, conversation, emotion, and artistic expression. If the long-term goals of the PRC include the establishment of unity and the maintenance of territorial integrity, then all local languages need to be actively fostered. The domains of language use need to be broadened rather than narrowed. Local linguistic resources must be combined with technical skills to create long-term research and development activity, as part of China's modernization of its Western Regions.

Policy Recommendations

China

All languages and cultures are intrinsically of high "quality"
Each and every human language is uniquely adapted to a social environment by its speakers. All languages, then, are of equal quality; all languages are up to the task of communication in any number of domains. Generally, the number of domains in which a language is spoken is one indicator of its vitality. If the lexicon of a language falls short in a given domain, language planners can systematically develop the lexicon in that semantic area. After all, Chinese language planners have excelled at lexicon development for Chinese in the domain of information technology vocabulary;[70] these techniques could simply be applied to minority languages in the domains of technology (information and infrastructural); international law; and economics. Using techniques honed during the dissemination of socialist political vocabulary during the 1950s, language planners for Xinjiang and other minority areas can ensure that these neologisms are incorporated into pedagogical materials and teaching at all educational levels.

Implement existing language-use policies

Though the 1984 Nationality Law and the Law on Regional Autonomy for minority nationalities clearly spell out the basic premises of linguistic rights for speakers of minority languages in China, the implementation of those laws has been weak. To allow minorities to maintain and develop their own languages, the current trend towards reducing minority-language use in education and the media must be reversed. The central and Autonomous Region governments should implement the 1984 minority cultural-policy directives and develop explicit language policies tailored to local sociolinguistic conditions. Future language planning on the scope of legal protections and language-maintenance efforts could refer to the *European Charter for Regional or Minority Languages* (Council of Europe 1999).

Enhance language domains for major minority languages

Education and the media constitute primary language domains. Publications and media should continue to be in both major minority languages and Chinese. Resources and talent need to be directed towards improving the quality of instruction and instructional materials in minority languages, which have been long overlooked by researchers and standardizing bodies. Governments and their standardizing bodies should work to expand language-use domains, particularly in the areas of media and of education. National-level policies promoting or hindering multilingualism in China should be re-evaluated by using case studies of successful language planning, such as efforts in the Baltic States or South Africa.

Consider a "three-language" policy for Inner Asia

Minority languages are a resource. As in India, China could commit resources to supporting three languages: (1) the national language (modern standard Chinese); (2) English; and (3) a regional language (e.g., Category II languages as defined in Figure 1, such as Standard Uyghur for Xinjiang or Lhasa Tibetan for Tibet).[71] Each of these languages serves a particular purpose. Mandarin Chinese unifies the nation and is necessary for intergroup communication within China, English allows China economic advantages in the global economy, and the regional languages maintain social stability and foster pride in ethnic heritage.

> *As in India, China could commit resources to supporting three languages*

Such a formula would not represent a radical change in Chinese language policy. Mandarin is already recognized as the national language, and the languages of titular minorities in the country's Autonomous Regions are already accorded *de jure* support in a number of linguistic domains. Where this formula does depart from current policy (overt and covert) is (1) in its explicit recognition of the importance of international languages; and (2) in its revival of measures to maintain and enhance the titular minority languages, such as Uyghur and Mongolian.

While this formula's implementation in India was flexible and wide-ranging, such a policy could be implemented in China first in Xinjiang only under strict central government control. If deemed successful, the formula could be applied to other Autonomous Regions.

It may appear counterintuitive to recommend language policy liberalization for China's most instable region. Yet this very instability indicates the urgent need for policy change.

Education: bilingualism and language sequencing

At a bare minimum, as Naran Bilik (n.d.) suggests, Uyghur language education should be provided at least to those tertiary institutions that train teachers, since most of these teachers will return to monolingual Uyghur areas. In addition to continued teacher training, textbooks in all subjects should be prepared in major minority languages in order to foster bilingualism through the primary, secondary, and tertiary levels. The need for minority-language textbooks in all subject areas (not merely language) is particularly urgent for primary levels. The costs of material preparation should be weighed against the current costs of unemployment among minority young people.

While planning for instructional languages is complex, some basic principles can be outlined here. During their nine mandatory years of education, pupils should receive a full nine years of education in their mother tongue (or best language). Pupils should also study other languages. The outline below proposes that all students have the same total number of years of language study, and that the languages a student studies be determined by her mother tongue and personal goals. Hans living in minority regions would study English as their second (and second-most important) language, the regional minority language as their third, and possibly another foreign language as their fourth language. Major minorities such as the Uyghurs would study Chinese and English simultaneously as their second languages. (There is plenty of precedence for the multiple study of additional languages in for example Germany.) Other minorities

Figure 4. Language Sequencing Options for Speakers in Minority Areas

		grades 1-3	4-6	7-9
Hans in minority areas (e.g., Urumchi)	Standard Chinese	■	■	■
	Regional min lang.			▓
	Other min lang.			
	English		▒	▒
	other foreign lang.			░
Major minorities (e.g., Uyghurs)	Standard Chinese		■	■
	Regional min. lang.	▓	▓	▓
	Other min. lang.			
	English			▒
	other foreign lang.			
Other minorities (e.g., Kazakhs) (option 1)	Standard Chinese		■	■
	Regional min. lang.		▓	▓
	Other min. lang.	■		
	English		░	░
	other foreign lang.			
Other minorities (option 2)	Standard Chinese		■	■
	Regional min. lang.			
	Other min. lang.	■		
	English		▒	▒
	other foreign lang.		░	░

such as Xinjiang Kyrgyz would have a choice about their second language: They could (a) study the regional minority language (e.g., Uyghur); or (b) start in on English as the second, and study another foreign language as their third language. Figure 4 indicates these sequences graphically. All pupils would have a minimum of six years of Mandarin Chinese (solid black shading in Figure 4) and a full nine years of their mother tongue.

Developing speaker language competencies in three critical languages—Chinese, English, and the native language—should be the aim for policy on nondominant language speakers.

These priorities would need input from the regional Education Commissions, parents, students, and a cross-section of Uyghurs. For example, the educational goals of families would certainly vary: For some, English may prove key to future employment, while for others, English might have little relevance. Adopting a multitiered system (see Figure 4) would address these differing needs while providing "a more equitable balance between real national requirements, social expectations, and resources (educational, economic)" (Gray 2003: 4).

Support the direct study of English and other foreign languages
Given the Indo-European vocabulary in most languages of Xinjiang and in regions such as Inner Mongolia, there is every reason to teach foreign languages to the region's minorities through the medium of major standard minority languages such as Uyghur and Mongolian. This would both add prestige to the local languages and allow foreign languages to be learned more efficiently, thus producing a more highly skilled workforce.

If Beijing has qualms about English overwhelming Chinese, it should look to the Indian experience. In that country, even the development of an English-style education did not upset the balance of majority and minority languages, since English was seen as a key to India's entry into the modern world (Schiffman 1999: 436). In China, English is a pragmatic tool for the 21st century. Hindering minority learning of foreign languages by using Chinese as the medium of instruction has already sown unnecessary discontent among minority youth there.

Will fostering minority cultures ultimately foster separatism?
Early PRC policies aimed at fostering economic development as well as cultural autonomy (i.e., language and "traditions") as much as possible, while limiting political autonomy. But since the 1990s, the PRC government has concluded that even cultural autonomy leads to separatist activity and is therefore dangerous. Yet the opposite is likely true: Between the mid-1980s and 1996, the CCP attained a grudging tolerance for its Xinjiang policies by a significant proportion of the Uyghur elites. But for many Uyghurs, after the 1996 "Strike Hard" campaign and China's calculated association of Islam in Xinjiang with international terrorism since 2001, acceptance and tolerance shifted to hatred. Eliminating Uyghur-language instruction in schools further eroded acceptance of Chinese rule. In targeting these core markers of Uyghur culture, previously slumbering sensitivities were inflamed. For language and religion are valued by most ordinary Uyghurs as central aspects of their identity. As both are considered inviolable and semi-private, significant encroachment by a dominant Chinese culture is perceived as an attack on identity.

Restrictions placed on minority cultural expression thus actually *foster* resistance. To maintain a stable nation-state and continue to develop the XUAR and the country, there is thus little other choice than to, at a minimum, support the *maintenance* of local languages and cultures if not their *revitalization*. The central government's concern that Xinjiang will become China's Kashmir is exaggerated. Ethnic pride is not the same as separatism; teaching Uyghur will support positive language attitudes. Prohibiting Uyghur-language teaching in an area as sensitive as Xinjiang will radicalize a portion of once-indifferent students, just as prohibiting ordinary mosque attendance for those under 18 may well create an interest in militant foreign Islam: both prohibitions create a "cause" for hotheaded young people.

> *The...concern that Xinjiang will become China's Kashmir is exaggerated*

China can strike a new balance between national security concerns and cultural autonomy. The country's leadership can demonstrate that its Xinjiang cultural policy is indirectly a counterterrorist measure by supporting moderate cultural expression and preventing linguistic and religious radicalization. Even the Uyghur language could be promoted for its intelligence-gathering potential in greater Central Asia.

Link language development with economic development
New information technologies (IT) can be used to create job skills through the use of both majority and minority Chinese languages. As such, these technologies would be a general economic stimulus. Equally importantly, IT research and development would enhance political stability in the region by recognizing and fostering the technical and linguistic skills of the large minority populations.

One major complaint in Xinjiang has been the utter lack of economic opportunities for Uyghurs, particularly college graduates. Beijing could go a long way to recovering the confidence and support of Xinjiang's urban intellectuals by establishing an information technology research and development center in Ürümchi, with a satellite in Kashgar or Ili.

Xinjiang's multilingualism is its asset; the bi- and trilingualism of educated Uyghurs, Sibes, Tatars, Kazakhs, and Kyrgyz (among other groups) can be put to use developing cutting-edge multimodal data architecture and tools, for example, voice-recognition and speech synthesis systems for Turkic languages and Chinese dialects other than standard Mandarin.

The array of languages in the competence of most of Xinjiang's minority population is particularly attractive for the development of IT products destined for the international market, particularly in Central Asia. China can specifically include IT in its program to develop its Western Regions; it can encourage foreign direct investment in language technologies.

Incorporate current sociolinguistic research in assessment
Recent sociolinguistic research has brought holistic methodologies to the investigation of speech communities. These include cost-benefit analyses of language policies in a multilingual context. Newer theoretical approaches can be applied to both *de jure* and *de facto* language policies. Diagnostic tools such as UNESCO's *Language Vitality and Endangerment* guidelines, which include nine criteria for language assessment (UNESCO 2003), can be employed to establish language-planning priorities.

This may well be the century of Chinese nationalism. If Chinese minorities are to participate in the modern Chinese nation, the PRC should foster their languages, for languages are central to national identity. There is now an opportunity for China's leadership to shape language policy so that it creates cooperation rather than resistance.

Changing elite and popular public perceptions of non-Hans
Enhancing Han acceptance of minority cultures benefits the nation as a whole. Without this acceptance, the continuing dichotomization of trusted Hans and "backward" minorities may deepen the rifts between ethnic groups in Xinjiang; minority nationalities such as the Uyghurs who see no future in participating in China's society may eventually decide to opt out.

it could be Han chauvinism that leads to a breakup of China

Indeed, it could be Han chauvinism that leads to a breakup of China.

Far from being simply about resources, the fundamental conflict includes an important emotional component. Minority resistance of any kind thrives on racism and bias, including bias against a local culture not being high enough "quality." Such resistance can be effectively neutralized, however, if minorities can be convinced that Chinese development in minority regions is primarily economic and does not include cultural annihilation.

Reintroducing more pluralistic cultural policies would in effect be mandating a change in attitudes towards the value of minority cultures. Shifting both policy and popular opinion would require a commitment of central and local government resources to minority media and education as well as winning over both policymakers and the general populace. Through the music of Mongolian and Tibetan pop stars singing in standard Chinese, there already exists a new if superficial interest on the part of young Hans towards major minorities.

Changing public perceptions from the central government level may also involve refining the concept of nationality (*minzu*) so that it is without stigma. Such categories served China well for nation building, but they need to be substantially revised over time for the long-term stability of China as a multicultural nation.

United States
The United States has pragmatic reasons that limit the extent to which it is willing to exercise influence regarding cultural policy in Xinjiang. Yet completely ignoring the cultural autonomy issue in Xinjiang could indirectly exacerbate violent extremism.

Before 2001, the United States was already reluctant to involve itself in China's internal affairs, since the PRC had already become an important political force and trading partner. The U.S. role in Chinese affairs was thus limited to that of an observer and commentator, largely on human rights issues. After September 2001, even the human rights commentary has become muted, as Washington's stated priority shifted to combating international terrorism. Furthermore, U.S.-China bilateral relations will continue to have much higher priority for Washington than do any Chinese domestic issues, be they matters of human rights, public health, or cultural autonomy, including linguistic and religious autonomy.

Clearly distinguish Uyghur nationalism from terrorism
Washington has competing bilateral and multilateral priorities in Xinjiang, much as Beijing must balance national stability with transnational considerations. The PRC's media have made good use of the unfortunately common misperception that Islam is monolithic and violent as well as of the American antiterrorism priority. Although the PRC has taken care to avoid labeling all Uyghurs as terrorists, its media rhetoric (using such terms as *Muslim Uyghurs, Uyghur terrorists, holy war,* and *Eastern Turkestan*) still insinuates that the Uyghurs constitute a long-term terrorist threat.

Washington, however, has signaled that its credulity has limits. Although the United States declared ETIM a terrorist organization in 2002, in the same year the U.S. Assistant Secretary for Democracy, Human Rights, and Labor stated in Ürümchi that human rights efforts would not be compromised by terrorism (Craner 2002).[72]

Assessing conflicts in Xinjiang from the viewpoint of international terrorism alone is dangerously simplistic. The United States should also take into consideration Chinese ethnopolitics and regional Central Asian geopolitics. The Chinese state has a critical interest in gaining influence in Central Asia and maintaining tight control of the Xinjiang territory. Limiting Uyghur nationalism in Xinjiang (and successfully encouraging Central Asian governments to do the same with their Uyghur populations) is merely a means to this end. Media reports labeling dissent in Xinjiang as terrorism have allowed the international community, particularly the Americans, to facilitate this territorial consolidation.

Assessing conflicts in Xinjiang from the viewpoint of international terrorism alone is dangerously simplistic

Just because Uyghurs are ethnonationalistic and Muslim does not automatically render them separatists, let alone terrorists. There is a small number of extremists within Xinjiang who do advocate independence from China, including by violence, but these extremists do not currently appear to be involved in international terrorist movements. There are others in Xinjiang who have no desire for a separate state, but advocate political and cultural reform. There are deeply religious Uyghurs and secular nationalists. But the vast majority of China's more than 8 million Uyghurs simply want to live respectable, comfortable lives. While most are willing to learn Chinese and adapt to Chinese society, many believe that Uyghur cultural accommodation should not be at the expense of their own language, beliefs, and traditions.

Though U.S. policy is actually more nuanced than it appears, there will be two negative consequences if the United States continues to give even the *impression* that it has jumped aboard China's repressive ship in Xinjiang:

- The Chinese government and media will be emboldened to step up demands for assistance in their own "war against terror," in the future even possibly requesting military assistance to quash nationalist unrest in Xinjiang; and
- Uyghurs (and most moderate Muslim Turkic speakers in the Central Asian republics) will come to resent the United States for its association with the clampdowns in Xinjiang, and the situation will radicalize these groups.

View Xinjiang not only as part of China, but also as part of Central Asia
Administratively, Xinjiang is firmly part of China, but it also has
strong cultural and geopolitical ties to Central Asia. Uyghurs, Kazakhs,
Kyrgyz, and other non-Han Chinese groups in Xinjiang share languages,
transnational ethnic identities, and religious beliefs with their neighbors
to the west. Many feel strongly that their history is tied to Central Asia,
harboring a feeling of kinship due to perceived common historical origins
and traditions. The kinship is also literal in some cases: Many Uyghurs have
relatives in the Central Asian republics.

Still, it would be a mistake to characterize the non-Han denizens of
Xinjiang as homogeneous with the peoples of the Central Asian republics.
The sense of kinship is nebulous and historicized; in modern day-to-day
life, neighboring ethnic groups are also likely to make sport of each others'
cherished traditions. Such lampooning is particularly common between
sedentary peoples (such as Uyghurs or Uzbeks) and formerly nomadic
peoples (such as Kazakhs or Kyrgyz).

The Chinese state, for its part, sees trade with the Central Asian
republics as a major way of gaining influence in the region, and plans to
increase its trade with that region by a factor of 50 in the next 10 years
(Swanström 2003). Any U.S. policy on Xinjiang should therefore consider
China's own national interests vis-à-vis its minorities and its Central Asian
neighbors.

Support increased cultural autonomy
China's relaxation of controls on minority cultural expression in the
1980s and 1990s was well-conceived; the current Chinese repression of
indigenous cultures is exacerbating ethnic conflict in Xinjiang. The United
States would do well to encourage China to see that supporting Xinjiang's
local languages and peaceful religious expression would be in China's best
interest. Under more tolerant policies, Uyghur moderates, whose support
the Chinese state is losing, would be more willing to accept Chinese rule.
Uyghur extremists—who are currently well positioned to gain new recruits
because of Chinese hard-line tactics—would then have virtually no support
within their communities.

Political and cultural stability (e.g., language maintenance) are
dependent on economic opportunities within Xinjiang. In northeastern
China, there has been a surge of interest in the Korean language prompted
by the success of South Korean business investments there (Bilik n.d.).
Would China allow the widespread teaching of Turkish, Central Asian

Turkic, and English in Xinjiang if the economic benefits of such tolerance could be demonstrated?

Specifically, the United States could urge China to (1) promote the maintenance and expansion of language domains for major minority languages, particularly in education and the media; (2) loosen restrictions on religious worship and instruction for all ages, both in the mosque and at home; (3) train and employ minority cadres who have real power, not just figurehead roles (cf. Yom 2002); (4) take steps—such as technology training—to reduce high Uyghur unemployment and employer bias against Uyghurs; and (5) pay special attention to the training of women (already one of China's strengths). In their dialogues with PRC officials, U.S. agencies should promote the development of significantly more cultural autonomy in Chinese border areas such as Xinjiang and Tibet.

Do not abandon existing China policies

The United States should clarify and maintain existing policies on trade, human rights, and Taiwan when these policies do not conflict with national security priorities. Beijing should be encouraged not to force Uyghurs to choose between ethnic loyalty and loyalty to the Chinese state. The Uyghur autonomy issue may have been recast as an international terrorist issue, but it should not distract the United States from its other priorities in China. Security aid should thus be clearly separated from development aid (cf. Siegle et al. 2004).

Recognize Uyghurs as important political allies of the United States and as Chinese citizens

Uyghurs were extremely pro-American—until the United States called them terrorists. Many Uyghurs hope that the United States can moderate the Chinese monoculturalist pressure in Xinjiang. While it is clear that Washington's primary ally must be the Beijing government, this alliance need not exclude major Chinese minorities such as the Uyghurs. It is critical that the United States cultivate a relationship with the Uyghurs, although also not to the exclusion of Beijing.

Uyghur Islam…[should be used] to educate Americans about diversity in Islam

Specifically, the United States should extend their support of peaceful cultural expression and development by facilitating study-abroad opportunities for Chinese minorities such as Uyghurs in the United States, including both visa processing and educational opportunities. The United States should also continue to support minority-language radio broadcasts.

Washington should also consider using Uyghur Islam as a case study to educate Americans about diversity in Islam. Uyghur Islam is very approachable; everyday life and religion are tightly bound. Furthermore, radical militant and/or fundamentalist Islam has had as yet very little influence in Xinjiang, in contrast to some of China's western neighbors. That Salafi/"Wahhabi" Islam has not caught on in Xinjiang clearly indicates that there is no support for Islamic extremism among the populace.

Ordinary Uyghurs have even less sympathy for international terrorism; even among extremists, relatively few Uyghurs have proved to have been involved in terrorist activities in Pakistan and Afghanistan. The Uyghurs' historically strongly pro-American stance renders claims that extremists were involved in attacking American targets highly implausible.[73] It is important not to equate Uyghurs with fundamentalist Islam or terrorism, and instead to remember that most every Uyghur simply wants to keep his or her traditions while participating in their local and modern world, just like anyone else.

Establish a consulate or trade center in Xinjiang

A civilian American presence in the XUAR would have both practical and outreach functions. A U.S. trade center in Xinjiang could facilitate doing business in western China; a consulate could alleviate pressures at the U.S. Embassy in Beijing, which currently serves all of north China. (At present, residents of Xinjiang must travel 4,000 kilometers at considerable cost just to reach the U.S. embassy in Beijing.) Either facility would have the potential to moderate Chinese heavy-handedness in the regions, such as the unnecessarily provocative joint Pakistan-China military exercises of the summer of 2004. Given that the PRC government is uneasy about U.S. bases in the Central Asia republics, a successful U.S. proposal on Xinjiang would stress the practical advantages of such an institution.

Endnotes

1. Translation by Chavannes (1907). I would like to thank Naran Bilik, Nathan Light, Stevan Harrell, the East-West Center Washington *The Dyanmics and Managing Internal Conflicts in Asia* March 2004 Study Group participants, and three reviewers for comments on this paper.

2. Norris et al. (1994); Statement of the Government of the People's Republic of China, July 29, 1996; Associated Press (Beijing), July 29, 1996; Reuters (Beijing), July 29, 1996.

3. Though other large minority groups in contiguous areas exist in China, these groups are either overwhelmingly semi-speakers of their heritage language (such as a sizeable portion of the approximately 16.2 million Zhuangs in Guangxi and environs) or heritage language non-speakers (such as the nearly 10.7 million Manchus in Manchuria). In contrast, China's northwest and southwest areas are, by conservative estimates, home to 27 million fully fluent non-Chinese native-language speakers (encompassing 80 percent of the total Mongolic, Turkic, and Tibetic populations). Most of these non-Han peoples, except those living in remote regions, speak at least some Chinese in addition to their native languages. Some groups, particularly those in the east (such as most Manchus), no longer speak their native languages. All population figures here are from the 2000 census unless otherwise indicated.

4. In contrast to *Xiyu*, *Xinjiang* ("New Dominion"), although also not free of imperial connotations, is in modern China a precise label for the territory of the eponymous Chinese Autonomous Region. Historically, *Xiyu* ("Western Regions") referred specifically to areas west of Yumen (the frontier Jade Gate) to the Pamirs, and northwest to what is now called Issyk Köl and Semireyche. An entire volume of the official *History of the Later Han Dynasty* (*Hou Han shu* (25–221 CE)), the *Xiyu juan,* is devoted to the Western Regions (see Hill 2002). Note that for economic development purposes, "the West" also includes the decidedly southern areas of Guangxi and Guizhou.

5. The overt/covert distinction, standard in language planning scholarship, implies neither a value judgment nor espionage. Overt/covert (which could also be termed explicit/implicit) policy is related to the *de jure/de facto* policy described below, in that covert language policy is the result of the application of social and political norms (of the elite, of the populace, or both) to official, overt policies.

6. The United States has never had a language standardization organization or an official language, although campaigns for the exclusive use of American English (e.g., the recent English-Only movement) periodically gain public attention. Covert U.S. language policy recognizes and promotes Latin American Spanish as a de facto second national language; American businesses have driven the covert promotion of Spanish, particularly in the economic domain. Still, American English is clearly dominant and enjoys higher prestige, and overt education policy has restricted Spanish to the status of a "transitional" language for monolingual Spanish speakers and a "foreign" language for all others.

7. There are 56 officially recognized *minzu* ("nationalities"), of which 55 are *shaoshu minzu* ("national minorities"). China is home to over a hundred unofficial ethnolinguistic groups, which are officially subsumed under *minzu*.

8. Non-prestige Han Chinese tend to be rural, poor and/or speaking a variety of Chinese other than the Standard Language (Mandarin Chinese). The Chinese lexeme *wenhua* ("culture, civilization") includes *wen*, the glyph denoting "written language." As many observers have pointed out previously, for Chinese elite society a central aspect of being cultured and civilized is having an orthography and being literate. Besides sheer numbers, one of the reasons that Uyghur is a relatively high-prestige language in China is precisely because of the long history of orthographies and literacy among the elite sedentary Turkic speakers of the Tarim Basin.

9. National minorities were identified in an exhaustive process according to the Stalinist criteria of having a common language, territory, economic life, and psychological make-up manifested in culture. During the 1950s, the central government sent out teams of linguists and anthropologists across China, often pairing them with local researchers. Eventually, in 1982, a total of 56 nationalities (55 national minorities and the Han) were officially recognized; this work also formed the basis for most of the important first grammatical and ethnographic sketches.

10. As early as 1975, however, there were isolated cases of language reform on non-Han languages, e.g. script reform for the Nuosu (Yi) of southwestern China (Harrell and Bamo 1998).

11. The term "barbarian minorities" corresponds to those unassimilated peoples historically termed "raw barbarians," while "sinicized minorities" corresponds to peoples who were partially assimilated to eastern Chinese culture. These partially assimilated peoples were known historically as "cooked barbarians" and included nonprestige Hans such as the Hakkas. See Harrell (1993) and Harrell (1995).

12. While Uyghur music does have complex Central Asian roots and commonalities with Middle Eastern music, it is not "Arabic." Press statements such as "Arabic music coming from a nearby building audibly demonstrates that Kashgar is closer to Baghdad than Beijing" (Lynch 2004) imply erroneously that Arab culture has a long-entrenched influence in the region, which only fuels the irrational and racist fear that radical Arab militants are infiltrating Xinjiang.

13. See for example Rudelson (1997). A similar insularity exists among some Yi groups; see Harrell and Li (2003).

14. For the Monguors of Qinghai (northern Tibet), who call themselves mostly Mangghuer and Mongghul, the Chinese ethnonym *Tu* is ambiguous; its basic meaning is "earth," as an ethnonym can mean simply "indigenous [person]," but it also connotes "hick." As part of another PRC ethnonym *Tujia*, the same lexeme *Tu* also connotes "convict," at least in the southern Chinese province of Guizhou (Brown 2001).

    Though ethnic groups in the Taiwan archipelago are not subject to PRC ethnic policy, they have nonetheless been conceptually subsumed under the PRC ethnic labeling system. Nine fully distinct ethnolinguistic Austronesian groups on Taiwan have been lumped under *gaoshan zu*, or "High Mountain nationality." (The Japanese term for the indigenous Austronesians on the Taiwanese archipelago, 高砂族 *takasagozoku* (cf. 高砂 *takasago* "Formosa"), was copied into Chinese as 高山（族）*gaoshan* (*zu*) during the second half of the Japanese colonial period, 1895–1945. See Encyclopedia Nipponica (2001). This label, originally neutral if inaccurate (half were originally flatlanders and some are island dwellers), has also taken on subtly deprecatory connotations. Calling indigenous Austronesians (Atayal, Tsou, etc.) "high mountain" people echoes the Turkish government's resolutely myopic designation of its Kurdish population until recently as "Mountain Turks." From "high mountain person" and "hick," it is not much of a mental leap to the terms "uncultivated" or "uncultured."

15. Sometimes, communicative domains for minority languages also literally shrank. It became commonplace, for example, for bilingual street and shop signs in Xinjiang to be written in large Chinese characters, with disproportionately tiny Uyghur letters above (the latter were termed "eyebrows" by Uyghur quipsters).

16. See for example Gupta (1970). As in China, local elites in India established a hierarchy of regional languages, so there was "good" Tamil (*centamir*) and "broken" Tamil (*koduntamir*). For more on this topic, see Shapiro and Schiffman (1981). I thank Arun Swamy for drawing my attention to this parallel.

17. See Sautman (1999). In education, minorities were granted preferential treatment on university entrance examinations; at Xinjiang University, for example, Hans had to score 100 points higher than minorities. An alleged poster protest by a Han professor criticizing the policy as being one of reverse discrimination resulted in the professor's removal, after Uyghur students supposedly "held rallies and demanded all Han students should have to take their entrance exams in Uyghur and see how well they would do" (Kostrzewa 1996: 189–90).

18. Named after Chagatay (d. 1242), the second son of Timur khan (Tamerlane). The Turko-Persian culture of Samarkand, Bukhara, Herat, Kokand, Khiva, and Kashgar flourished between the 14th and 19th centuries; the Turkic language and literatures of these elites came to be known as Chagatay. Both Uyghurs and Uzbeks claim the great 11th c. philologist Mahmud al-Kashgari, author of the three-volume *Divan lugat at-türk* (Compendium of the Turkic Dialects) as their own.

19. Numbering over 20,000 in the early 20th century, the Tatar population has dwindled in the last 100 years. Tatars, originally sedentary relatives of the Noghays who came to the Junggarian Basin during the 19th century (though some as early as the 10th c.), were merchants, handworkers, and landed farmers who fled the Tsarist and later Soviet crackdowns. Having become Muslim earlier than Uyghurs and Kazakhs, Tatars were seen as knowledgeable on religious matters; as immigrants from Russian territories, many introduced European elements into the cities at the foothills of the Tian Shan mountains (cf. Hoppe 1998).

20. The term *minzu* ("nationality") is now for all intents and purposes an abbreviated form of *shaoshu minzu* ("minority nationality"); in theory, however, *minzu* originally *included* Han Chinese groups.

21. The ethnolinguistic hierarchy is reproduced neatly in graphic images of nationalities that grace the Chinese currency. All whole-currency denominations (1–100 *Renminbi*, or RMB) feature major nationalities with populations of at least five million each. At the top of the pyramid on the highest-denomination bill (the 100 RMB note) is the ur-Han Chinese leader, Chairman Mao. The 10-yuan note features nationalities at the next level down: Mongolian and Han farmers, the latter pictured more prominently. They represent Category II (Regional Linguae Francae), although given the Han farmer's well-scrubbed but rustic appearance, he likely speaks a low-prestige Category III variety of Chinese. The 5 *yuan* note pictures a Hui (Chinese Muslim) man and Tibetan woman (both Category III); the 2 *yuan* note has Category II Yi and Uyghur women; the one *yuan* has Category III Yao and Dong women; the five *jiao* (*mao*) note has Miao and Zhuang women (Miao is Category III; the Zhuang ethnolinguistic complex is theoretically Category II due to sheer population (15 million), although most but not all Zhuang groups have lost their language, see Kaup 2000), the two *jiao* note Buyi (Category IV) and Korean women (Category III, but a comparatively small population), and the one *jiao* note features "Gaoshan" (Category IV) and Manchu men. Manchus, despite their population of 10 million, never recovered their 19th-century status as a prestige ethnolinguistic group. They therefore anchor the smallest, now nearly worthless piece of paper currency, together with a putative group that exists only within the imagined boundaries of the PRC.

22. Examples of such minor languages (in a political sense) are Sibe and Salar, explored in Dwyer (1996).

23. Even 25 years later, orthographic reform was the primary preoccupation of the central government's language researchers, as a 1978 conversation between the director of the Beijing-based nationalities Language Research Institute and the former Swedish Ambassador Gunnar Jarring reveals: "the institute's most important task...[was] to work out written languages for the different minorities." (Jarring 1986: 14).

24. *Old Uyghur* primarily describes the language of the Turfan kingdom of the 9th and 14th centuries C.E. Chinggis Khan learned the Sogdian script beginning in 1204 from a captured Uyghur scholar named Tatatunggha (*History of the Yuan dynasty* vol. 124, Biography of Ta-ta-tung-a). Among the Mongols, this instance is the first known mention of written language (Jagchid and Hyer 1979: 210). The historical Uyghurs had themselves acquired the script via Nestorian Christians.

25. The monk 'Phags-pa wrote, "When we record matters, we use the Chinese and Uighur script to express the language of our dynasty.... We lack a satisfactory system to express our written language" (*History of the Yuan dynasty* vol. 202, Biography of Ba-si-ba ['Phags pa]; in Jagchid and Hyer: 212). That Chinese was employed as the default Inner Asian script is attested in the lexicon of Inner Asian languages: Words having to do with writing and writing implements are of Chinese origin (e.g., Mongolian *bichig* ("writing"), and Salar *pite-* ("to write") are both derived from Middle Chinese "writing brush").

26. During a closed meeting in May and June 1921 in Tashkent, the 9th century term *Uyghur*, denoting pre-Muslim Turkic speakers, was revived as the formal ethnonym for the oasis dwelling southeastern Turkic speakers of the area. The meeting included a delegation of Eastern Turkestanis from Ili and Kashgar (Malov 1934).

27. The official spelling for the Autonomous Region includes the ethnonym *Uygur*; otherwise, we refer to the ethnolinguistic group as *Uyghur*.

28. The first Uyghur language-planning meetings in the world were held in 1925 in Samarkand and 1928 in Almaty, at a time when Uyghur speakers were still using essentially the Arabic-based Chagatay script. Switching to a Latin-based script was discussed at the first meeting and formally adopted at the second (Nadzip 1970, cited in Bruchis 1988).

29. Interviews on script preferences were conducted in 1992, 1993, 1999, and 2000 in Ürümchi, Ghulja, Kashgar, Turfan, Aqsu, and environs. Sinophone Muslims are known as *Dunggan* in Xinjiang and west of the Pamirs, but termed *Hui* by the Chinese government.

30. Although work on an alphabetic transliteration system for Standard Chinese was initiated with the founding of the PRC in October 1949, the final official version was not adopted until nearly a decade later in February 1958, entitled *Hanyu pinyin fang'an* (Chinese phonetics scheme). Typical of the egalitarian idealism of those early days, the public was encouraged to submit alphabetic schemes and was again consulted in 1956–57 for a revision of the original draft (cf. DeFrancis 1977). This kind of participatory linguistics was a luxury that national minority-language policymakers could apparently not afford; during the same nine-year period, by contrast, some of China's largest national minority groups adopted and abandoned several entire orthographies, all without widespread public consultation. In Xinjiang, the sluggishness to introduce the Latin script for Uyghur and Kazakh was blamed on sabotage by the Gang of Four (Jarring 1986: 29).

31. See Jarring (id.); Bellér-Hann (1991): 73; and Wei (1993). For a discussion of the recent script changes in Xinjiang, see Sugawara (2001).

32. This bilingual dictionary was reissued in an Arabic-script edition in 2000.

33. The so-called national Language Romanization (*Gwoyeu Romatzyh*, i.e., *Guoyu Luomazi*) was approved in 1928 by the government but never used, except in some textbooks in the United States before 1979. Ironically, another orthography Latinized New Script (*Latinxua sin wenz*, i.e., *Ladinghua xin wenzi*) was created in 1929 and employed by 10,000 Chinese speakers in Soviet Central Asia.

34. Jarring (1986): 25. In 1978, no published history was available in the Uyghur language, nor were there any classes about Uyghur history. Educators explained to Ambassador Jarring that "there was only a course in Chinese history; more did not matter, since the history of Sinkiang was part of the history of China" (id.: 29).

35. In contrast, India had a 65 percent increase, and the United States had only a 26 percent increase (International Telecom Statistics 2000, Siemens workgroup, and Nua Internet Surveys 2000, in von Baratta (2000): XXXVI.

36. Thus, even though *Xinjiang* is a relatively high-frequency lexeme in the media, many Internet posters will render this as *Shinjang*. An example is Abdireyim (2003).

37. European/Turkish-style orthographies require some glyphs not found on the English-layout QWERTY keyboards used in China: ä, ü, ö, ç, ğ. These glyphs are also rendered as *ae/e, ue/u, oe/o, ch,* and *gh/g,* respectively.

38. Although Uyghur computing gained momentum in the 1990s, the first known Uyghur program was an Arabic-script utility created by Xinjiang University in 1989 (Sugawara 2001: 24).

39. Unicode was designed to be a universal 16-bit character set that was to cover all major modern written languages. Each character was to have exactly one encoding (code point). Unicode is not a glyph encoding—i.e. it is not a font, but rather specifies a standard for fonts. The ISO/IEC standards were developed to be compatible with existing character codes (e.g., previous GB [*guobiao*] codes or ASCII).

40. Weinreich (1945). The original statement, often misattributed to the linguist Uriel Weinreich, read in Yiddish: "A shprakh iz a diyalekt mit an armey un a flot."

41. Osmanov (1989). Chinese linguists recognize three dialects. Other linguists have used the following dialect names: Kashgar-Yarkand (Kashi-Shache); Yengi Hissar (Yengisar); Khotan-Keriyä (Hotän-Yutian); Chärchän (Qarqan, Qiemo); Aqsu (Aqsu); Qarashahr (Karaxahar); Kucha (Kuqa); Turfan (Turpan); Kumul (Hami); Ili (Kulja, Yining, Taranchi); Ürümchi (Ürümchi); Lopnor (Lopnur); Dolan; and Akto Türkmen. Those language varieties in the north are more influenced by modern Chinese.

42. Thanks to Stevan Harrell for the second example.

43. These might be termed *pushmi-pullyu* policies, after Hugh Lofting's fictional creature with heads facing in both directions.

44. Some scholars consider Turkic to be part of a larger Altaic family, which also comprises two other important families of Inner Asia: Mongolic and Manchu-Tungusic. Altaic languages display many structural similarities; other scholars would argue that these commonalities are due to contact-induced borrowing rather than a "genetic" (family) relationship. The differences that do exist between Uyghur, Kazakh, and Kyrgyz on either side of the border are largely differences of copied vocabulary (from Chinese or Russian) and pronunciation.

45. Since 2004, these sentences have been appearing weekly on the Language and Script Committee's website (www.xjyw.gov.cn/han/han.htm). The sample sentence of the week of June 12, 2004, as it had been the television show, was: "How are you? Nice to meet you."

46. For examples of these textbooks, see *Jichu Weiyu* (Basic Uyghur) (Ürümchi: Xinjiang University Press, 1991); and a different and equally good *Jichu Weiwueryu* (Basic Uyghur) (Beijing: Central Nationalities Institute Press, 1991).

47. HSK is also, of course, used for the assessment of foreign students along the lines of other standardized assessment tests such as the TOEFL (Test of English as a Foreign Language).

48. See *Zhonghua Renmin Gongheguo minzu quyu zizhifa / Law of the People's Republic of China on Regional Autonomy* (Beijing: Minzu, 2001): 49.

49. Minority students receiving a Chinese-language education are known in Xinjiang as *Min kao Han* (literally, "minorities testing Chinese").

50. These are the personal observations of the author, who had a child enrolled there from 1991 to 1993.

51. Gunnar Jarring (1986: 157) reported two and a half decades earlier in 1978 that only one-half of the teachers at the Kashgar elementary- and secondary-teacher training seminary could understand and speak Chinese.

52. Fezulla (1988) provides a small *English-Uighur Dictionary*, but it desperately needs expanding and updating. St. John (1993) edited a useable *Uighur-English Dictionary*. Both were reviewed in Dwyer (1994). Recently, a Chinese-English-Uyghur technical dictionary has appeared; see Xinjiang University (2003).

53. Ronald Gray (2003: 4), a long-term ESL teacher in China, recommends "the adoption of a two-tier educational system whereby those students who are both interested in, and demonstrate an ability, to learn English, would be allowed to pursue a special track English education program or school. For others, they could be taught a language (it does not have to be English) for a couple of years in junior high or high school so that they have a rudimentary knowledge of a language besides their own."

54. Thirteen of these include at least some publications in Uyghur (Imin and Musa 2001). The most important publishing houses in Xinjiang are: Xinjiang (XJ) People's Press (*Shinjang Xälq Näshriyati/Xinjiang Renmin chubanshe*); XJ Youth Press (*Sh. yashlar-ösmürlär näshriyati/XJ Qingshaonian chubanshe*); XJ Education Press (*Sh. ma'arip näshriyati/*XJ Jiaoyu chubanshe); Xinjiang University Press (*Shinjang uniwersiteti nähriyati/*XJ *daxue chubanshe*), and Kashgar Uyghur Press (*Qäshqär Uyghur näshriyati/Kashi Weiwuerwen chubanshe*). All but the last are based in Ürümchi. Nationalities Press (*Minzu chubanshe/Millätlär näshriyati*) in Beijing continues to publish many important Uyghur-language work materials, especially reference works.

55. There are also a very few local papers in local languages, such as the weekly Sibe-language *Chapchal News*, written entirely in Sogdian-script Sibe (in Chinese, *Xibo*) and in existence since 1946.

56. The earliest multi-purpose printing press was used by the Swedish mission in Kashgar between 1912 and 1938. It was employed to print news, literary works, advertisements, contracts, and even paper currency circulated in the area at the time, as well as missionary tracts. Before then, books were handwritten or imported from Tashkent, Samarkand, and Bukhara as far more expensive lithographs (Jarring 1991).

57. Al-Kashgari's three-volume dictionary was published in a modern Uyghur edition (1980) and a Chinese edition (2002). Scholarly attention was lavished on Yusuf Khas Hajip's *Qutadghu bilik*, for which a Sogdian script edition and the Ferghana version of the Arabic-script edition have appeared (1985), in addition to a modern standard Uyghur translation (in Arabic and Latin script on facing pages, 1984); and *Qädimki Uyghur yeziqdiki Maytri Simit* (Yüsüp et al. 1987). For a more complete annotated bibliography, see Light 1998a.

58. See www.uyghur.net/.

59. Across their empires, Chinese dynasties have a long tradition of substituting their own toponyms for local ones. Sometimes these are toponyms of a completely different meaning: for example, *Gongliu* (a Chinese surname + the sound *ra*) for *Toqquztara* ("Nine Growers") in western Xinjiang. Sometimes, the substitutions are simply taking a local toponym and rendering it pronounceable in Chinese: e.g., *Kashi* (which has no meaning in Chinese) for *Kashgar* ("enamel center"). Less frequently, a compromise approach is employed, in which historically imposed toponyms are nativized within the daunting constraints of Mandarin syllable structure: e.g., the regional capital *Dihua* has become *Wulumuqi* (also written as *Urumqi* and *Ürümchi*). Recent proposals in 2001 to standardize Uyghur surnames would also have a pragmatic impetus (i.e., the legally-binding transliteration of names) but are being met with similar suspicion.

60. Since at least the early 20th century, Uyghur nationalists have repeatedly employed *Eastern Turkestan* to refer to an imagined independent sedentary Turkic state encompassing the Tarim and Junggarian Basins, after the two short-lived independent republics of Eastern Turkestan (Kashgar in 1933 and Ili in 1944). In this not only separatist but also profoundly romanticized vein, the 1990s witnessed the emergence of an "Islamic Party of Eastern Turkestan" (which claimed responsibility for the Baren township riots in 1990) and the "Islamic Reformist Party of Eastern Turkestan."

61. A more comprehensive search, which is beyond the scope of the current study, would take into account the year that the web page was last updated, and would compare results from a variety of specialized and generalist search engines.

62. The kinship metaphor, which has its roots in the early 20th century, is enshrined in Article 50–3 of the Interim Constitution (Common Program), which was adopted on Sept. 29, 1949, and read in part: "…the People's Republic of China will become a big fraternal and cooperative family composed of all its nationalities" (Zhonghua…falü huibian 1985).

63. Separatists were alleged to have established schools and put up leaflets and posters advocating Xinjiang independence (Xu and Zhang 1997).

64. If we engage here in a different kind of splittism, namely of hairs, we may note that a "jihad mentality" necessarily implies a movement to rid an area of *all* unbelievers—yet we do not see the Uyghurs getting rid of the Mongols in Xinjiang.

65. *New York Times* (2002). Though the Department of State took pains to distinguish the estimated 20 to 200 individuals who were allegedly involved in a terrorist organization from the other 10 million Uyghurs, press coverage mentioning "Muslim Uyghurs" and "terrorists" in the same paragraph has served to equate the two in the minds of the public. A further problem in public perception concerns the timing of this terrorism listing. In August 2002, shortly before ETIM was added to the list, the U.S. government announced that it had obtained China's active support in the "war on terrorism." The coincidence of a "Uyghur terrorism" listing with China's sudden readiness to fight "international terrorism" hinted at a quid pro quo: China would help the United States if the United States helped China with its separatist problem. Though this coincidence is apparently misleading (the Department of State had delayed by several months announcing China's participation in anti-terrorist campaigns), public suspicion in Xinjiang and the West that Beijing and Washington are colluding against the Uyghurs will not dissipate overnight. See Millward (2004).

66. A Google™ search on June 13, 2004 for the co-occurring terms "Uyghur/Uighur/Uygur" and "Muslim terrorist" returned 92 citations.

67. "Since the Sept. 11 attacks..., Chinese diplomats have tried to convince foreign visitors that as many as 1,000 *Chinese Muslims* have trained in bin Laden's terrorist camps in Afghanistan" (Anonymous 2002, emphasis added). The sinophone Muslim Hui are obviously not meant here.

68. "...The Uyghur Islamic ethnic group [comprises] the majority of the population. 'Terrorism is the common enemy of the USA and China,' announced Colonel Luo Yan, Director of the Division of Strategic Studies at the Chinese Academy of Military Sciences" (Blume 2001). German translations are the author's.

69. The use of Eastern Turkestan, however, peaked in English in 2001 and 2003.

70. The coining of Chinese terms for computing vocabulary occurred largely in the early 1990s; that this lexicon is still in flux (i.e. not yet standardized) can be seen in computing dictionaries, which list two or three alternatives for one English term. See for example Zhang (1996).

71. The Indian three-language policy was implemented under widespread protests. Yet in the end, local Indian regions, depending on the degree of majority ethnonationalism, have had the flexibility to substitute a second local language for English, or to nearly ignore local languages entirely (Schiffman 1999: 436).

72. The U.S. stance was made explicit "after a meeting on December 6, 2001 with Chinese Vice Foreign Ministers Li Zhaoxing and Wang Yi, [when] US Ambassador Francis Taylor contended, 'The legitimate economic and social issues that confront the people in Western China are not necessarily terrorist issues and should be resolved politically rather than using counterterrorism methods'" (Yom 2003).

73. Washington gave the Foreign Terrorist Organization designation to tiny ETIM (cf. note 64) based on captured members' plans to attack the U.S. Embassy in Kyrgyzstan. If these plans were authentic, the motivation of the groups is perplexing, since Uyghurs would stand to gain nothing by blowing up a U.S. embassy. Uyghurs look to the United States as a potentially moderating influence in the region, and they are well aware that attacking U.S. embassies is hardly a way to curry favor with the Americans.

Bibliography

Abdireyim. 2003. *Uyghur Latin Élipbesi* (Uyghur Latin Alphabet). Accessed online at http://bilik.jahee.com/images/abc.gif and http://www.izbasar.net/news/list.asp?unid=151, on Nov. 11, 2004.

Alexander, Louis.G., ed. 1967. *New Concept English* (*Xin gainian Yingyu*). Beijing: Longman/Foreign Language Teaching and Research.

Announcing the Trial Implementation of HSK in National Minority Schools. 1997. Beijing: Education Commission. Cited in Bilik (n.d.).

Anonymous. 2002a. "English Craze Leaders." *China Today* (May). Accessed online at www.chinatoday.com.cn/English/e20025/e1.htm, on Nov. 11, 2004.

Anonymous. 2002b. "Medias: les chaines nationales." *Interex.* Accessed online at www.interex.fr/serv/frame_dynamique.asp?url=/ATLAS/interex/frame_atlas.asp?atlas_bd_infos=11&nom_theme=media, on Nov. 11, 2004.

Anonymous. 2002c. "China Claims Bin Laden Connections With Uighur Militants." *Emergency Response and Research News: Counterterrorism* (Jan. 22): 3. Accessed online at www.emergency.com/cntrter3.htm, on Nov. 11, 2004.

Ash, Lucy. 2002. "China's fearful Muslim minority." *BBC News* (Jan. 8). Accessed online at http://news.bbc.co.uk/1/hi/world/asia-pacific/1748801.stm, on Feb. 25, 2004.

Aubin, Françoise. 1998. "L'arrière-plan historique du nationalism Ouïgour, le Turkestan oriental des origines au XXe siècle." *Cahiers d'études sur la Méditeranée orientale et le monde turco-iranien* 25 (January–June).

British Broadcasting Corporation (BBC). 1998. "Jiang says hard work still needed to counter separatism." *BBC Online* (Mar. 7). Accessed online at http://news.bbc.co.uk/1/hi/world/monitoring/63005.stm, on Feb. 25, 2004.

Bellér-Hann, Ildikó. 1991. "Script Changes in Xinjiang." In Shirin Akiner, ed., *Cultural Change and Continuity in Central Asia.* London & New York: Kegan Paul International.

Bilik, Naran. n.d. "Schooling civil society among China's minorities: Language, ethnicity and internal frontiers." In Veronique Benei, ed. *Manufacturing Citizenship: Education and nationalism in Europe, South Asia, China*. London and New York: Routledge, forthcoming.

Blume, Georg. 2001. "Krisengewinnler China." *Die Zeit* 39.

Blume, Georg. 2002. "Interview: 'Wir wollen wie die anderen sein.'" *Die Zeit* 46.

Brown, Melissa J. 2001. "Ethnic Classification and Culture: The Case of the Tujia in Hubei, China." *Asian Ethnicity* 2, no. 1: 55–72.

Bruchis, Michael. 1988. *The USSR: Language and Realities*. Boulder, Co.: East European Monographs, CCL: 141.

Chavannes, Édouard. 1907. "Les pays d'Occident d'après le Heou Han chou." *T'oung pao* 8: 220.

Chung, Chien-peng. 2002. "China's War on Terror: September 11 and Uighur Separatism." *Foreign Affairs* (July/August).

Council of Europe. 1992. *European Charter for Regional or Minority Languages*. Accessed online at http://conventions.coe.int/Treaty/en/Treaties/Html/148.htm, on Nov. 11, 2004.

Craner, Lorne. 2002. "Craner Says Government Can't Ignore Human Rights in War on Terrorism" (speech delivered Dec. 19 at Xinjiang University). Accessed online at http://hongkong.usconsulate.gov/uscn/state/2002/121901.htm, on Nov 11, 2004.

DeFrancis, John. 1977. "Language and Script Reform in China." In *Advances in the Creating and Revision of Writing Systems*, ed. Joshua A. Fishman. The Hague: Mouton: 121–48.

Duan, Xinran. 2003. "Chinese Higher Education Enters a New Era." *Academe* (Nov.–Dec.): 22–27.

Dwyer, Arienne. 1994. "Materials for the Study of Modern Uyghur published in China." *Central Asiatic Journal* 38, no. 2: 155–59.

Dwyer, Arienne M. 1998. "The Texture of Tongues: Languages and Power in China." In William Safran, ed., *Nationalism and Ethno-regional Identities in China*. London: Frank Cass: 68–85.

Dwyer, Arienne M. 1996. "When orthographies are *verboten*: Endangered-language policy in northwestern China." In Garland D. Bills, ed. *Southwest Journal of Linguistics Special issue: Language Loss and Public Policy II*, vol.15, no. 1/2.

Embassy of the People's Republic of China in the United States of America. 2003. "History and Development of Xinjiang, Part 6." *Chinese Government White Paper*. Accessed online at www.china-embassy.org/eng/zt/zfbps/t36556.htm, on Nov. 11, 2004.

Encyclopedia Nipponica. 2001. *Kogakukan*. Accessed online at a non-static URL via the Japan Knowledge Database, on Aug. 25, 2004.

Erdem, Muhemmed. 2003. "Yeziq Ozgertixmu yaki yeziq birlikke kelturuxmu?" (Should the orthography be reformed, or should the orthography be standardized?). Accessed online at www.f20.parsimony.net/forum36933/messages/3410.htm, on Nov. 11, 2004.

Ershidin, Tursun. 2003. "Yeziq özgertix birdinbir ciqix yolimu?" (Is orthographic reform the only way out?). *Shinjang Geziti* (Xinjiang Daily), Mar. 9.

Fezulla, Änwär ed. 1988. *English-Uighur Dictionary*. Ürümchi: Xinjiang renmin.

FlorCruz, Haime. 2001. "China's dilemma in the fight against terrorism." *CNN* (Sept. 19). Accessed online at www.cnn.com/2001/WORLD/asiapcf/east/09/19/ret.china.dilemma/, on Nov. 11, 2004.

Fok, Anthony (compiler). 2002. "Application of IANA Charset Registration for GB18030." Accessed online at www.iana.org/assignments/charset-reg/GB18030, on Nov. 11, 2004.

Gray, Ronald. 2003. Review of McKay, Sandra Lee (2002), *Teaching English As An International Language: Rethinking Goals and Perspectives* (New York: Oxford University Press). In *TESL-TJ: Teaching English as a Second or Foreign Language* 7, no. 1 (June), R5: 1–4. Accessed online at www-writing.berkeley.edu/TESL-EJ/ej25/r5.html, on Nov. 11, 2004.

Große, Karl. 2002. "Kein Studium in Muttersprache: Peking schaltet Uigurisch ab." *Frankfurter Rundschau* (June 4): 2.

Gupta, Jyotirindra Das. 1970. *Language Conflict and National Development: Group Politics and National Language Policy in India*. Berkeley: UC Berkeley.

Hajib, Yusuf Khass. 1985. *Qutadghu bilik* (Sogdian-based Old Uyghur script facsimile edition, Vienna manuscript). Ürümchi: Xinjiang renmin.

Hajip Yusuf Khass. 1985. *Qutadghu bilik* (Arabic script edition). Ürümchi: Xinjiang renmin.

Hajip Yusuf Khass. 1986. *Qutadghu bilik* (Modern standard Uyghur translation). Beijing: Minzu.

Harrell, Stevan. 1993. "Linguistics and hegemony in China." *International Journal of the Sociology of Language* 103.

Harrell, Stevan. 1995. "Introduction: Civilizing Projects and the Reaction to Them." In *Cultural Encounters on China's Ethnic Frontiers*, ed. Stevan Harrell. Seattle & London: University of Washington: 3–36.

Harrell, Stevan, and Bamo Ayi. 1998. "Chinese Nationalism in Minority Language Textbooks: The Case of the Nuosu (Yi) of Liangshan." *Bulletin of the Concerned Asian Scholars* 30, no. 2: 62–71.

Harrell, Stevan, and Li Yongxiang. 2003. "The History of the History of the Yi, part II." *Modern China* 29, no. 3.

Hashimoto, Mantaro J. 1984. "Origin of the East Asian Linguistic Structure: Latitudinal Transitions and Longitudinal Developments of East and Southeast Asian Languages." *Computational Analyses of Asian and African Languages* 24: 35–42.

Hashimoto, Mantaro J. 1986. "The Altaicization of Northern Chinese." In *Contributions to Sino-Tibetan Studies*, ed. John McCoy and Timothy Light. Leiden: Brill.

Heberer, Thomas. 2000. "Some Considerations on China's Minorities in the 21st Century: Conflict or Conciliation?" Duisburg: *Duisburger Arbeitspapiere Ostasienwissenschaften* 31.

Hill, John E. (translator). 2002. "The Western Regions according to the *Hou Hanshu.*" Accessed online at http://depts.washington.edu/uwch/silkroad/texts/hhshu/hou_han_shu.html, on Feb. 20, 2004.

Hoppe, Thomas. 1998. *Die ethnischen Gruppen Xinjiangs: Kulturunterschiede und interethnische Beziehungen.* Hamburg: Mitteilungen des Instituts für Asienkunde 290: 478–479.

Imin, Yasin, and Batur Musa. 2001. "The Utilization of Computers in Uighur Publishing." *ABD* 31, no. 3: 8–9. Accessed online at www2.accu.or.jp/09/pdf31-3/31-3p08-9.pdf, on Feb. 20, 2004.

Information Office of the State Council of the People's Republic of China. 1999a. "A United Multiethnic Country." In *National Minorities Policy and Its Practice in China.* Beijing. Accessed online at http://english.peopledaily.com.cn/whitepaper/1(1).html, on Nov. 11, 2004.

Information Office of the State Council of the People's Republic of China. 1999b. "People's Daily Adherence to Equality and Unity Among Ethnic Groups." *In National Minorities Policy and Its Practice in China.* Beijing. Accessed online at http://english.peopledaily.com.cn/whitepaper/1(2).html, on Nov. 11, 2004.

International Organization for Standardization (ISO). 1995. ISO/IEC JTC 1/SC 2/WG 2 proposal (June). Accessed online at http://std.dkuug.dk/JTC1/SC2/WG2/docs/n1299.html, on Nov. 11, 2004.

Jagchid, Sechin, and Paul Hyer. 1979. *Mongolia's Culture and Society.* Boulder: Westview Press.

Jarring, Gunnar. 1991. *Prints from Kashgar.* Stockholm: Swedish Research Institute in Istanbul Transactions, Vol. 3.

Jarring, Gunnar. 1986. *Return to Kashgar.* Durham, NC: Duke University.

Jarring, Gunnar. 1981. "The New Romanized Alphabet for Uighur and Kazakh and Some Observations on the Uighur Dialect of Kashgar." *Central Asiatic Journal* 25, nos. 3–4: 230–45.

al-Kashgari, Mahmud. *Divan lugat at-türk* (Compendium of the Turkic Dialects). Modern Uyghur edition (Xinjiang renmin, 1980); Chinese edition (Beijing: Minzu, 2002).

Katzman, Kenneth. 2002. "Terrorism: Near Eastern Groups and State Sponsors, 2002." *CRS Report for Congress.* Accessed online at www.fas.org/irp/crs/RL31119.pdf, on Jan. 21, 2004.

Kaup, Katherine. 2000. *Creating the Zhuang: Ethnic politics in China.* Boulder: Lynne Rienner.

Kostrzewa, Thomas. 1996. *Separatist nationalism in Xinjiang* (unpublished doctoral dissertation). South Bend: University of Notre Dame.

Kurlantzick, Joshua. 2004. "Repression and Revolt in China's Wild West." *Current History* (Sept.): 262–67.

Landau, Jacob M., and Barbara Kellner-Heinkele. 2001. *Politics of Language in the ex-Soviet Muslim States: Azerbayjan, Uzbekistan, Kazakstan, Kyrgyzstan, Turkmenistan and Tajikistan.* London: Hurst.

Laponce, J.A. 1987. *Languages and their Territories.* Toronto: University of Toronto Press.

Li Lin. 2000. "The People's Republic of China." In *Language Policies and Language Education. The impact in East Asian Countries in the Next Decade*, ed. Ho Wah Kam & Ruth Y. L. Wong. Singapore: Times Academic Press: 79–96.

Li Sen. 1953. "Weiwuer wenzi gaige wenti" (Issues in Uyghur orthographic reform). In *Guonei shaoshu minzu yuyan wenzi gaikuang* (The State of Orthographic Reform for Domestic Minority Languages). Beijing: Zhongguo Yuwen.

Li Zengxiang, ed. 1992. *Tujueyu gailun* (Theories on the Turkic Languages). Beijing: Central Minorities College.

Light, Nathan. 1998a. "Imagining the Uyghur Literary Tradition." Accessed online at www.utoledo.edu/~nlight/bookcoll.htm, on Nov. 11, 2004.

Light, Nathan. 1998b. *Slippery Paths: The performance and canonization of Turkic literature and Uyghur muqam song in Islam and modernity*. Indiana University Ph.D. dissertation. Accessed online at www.utoledo.edu/~nlight/frntmtr1.htm, on Nov. 11, 2004.

Liu, E, and He Run. 1989. *Minzu lilun he minzu zhengce gangyao* (Essentials of Nationality Theory and Nationality Policy). Beijing: Central Nationalities Institute: 222–34.

Lynch, David J. 2004. "In Xinjiang Province, an uneasy coexistence." *USA Today* (Sept. 22).

Malov, S. E. 1934. "Materialy po uigurskim narechiyam Sin'dzyam" (Material on Uyghur of the peoples of Xinjiang). *Sbornik v chest'akad. S.F. Ol'denburga*. Leningrad: 307.

Mätniyaz, Razzaq, and Mirzakerim In'amshah, eds. 1991. *Uyghur tilidin asas/Jichu Weiwueryu* (Elementary Uyghur). Ürümchi: Xinjiang Jiaoyu.

Millward, James. 2004. "Violent Separatism in Xinjiang: A Critical Assessment." *Policy Studies* 6. Washington, DC: East-West Center Washington.

New York Times. 2002. "China Separatists' Allies 'Planned Attack.'" (Aug. 30).

Norris, Robert S., Andrew Burrows, and Richard Fieldhouse. 1994. *Nuclear Weapons Databook. Vol 5: British, French, and Chinese Nuclear Weapons*. Ballinger.

Osmanov, Mirsultan, and Abdurishid Sabit. 1987. *Hazirqi zaman Uyghur ädäbiy tilining imlasi häqqidä sewät* (An Collection on the Orthographic Rules of the Uyghur Literary Language). Ürümchi: Renmin.

Osmanov, Mirsultan. 1989. *Hazirqi zaman Uyghur tili di'alektliri* (The Dialects of Modern Uyghur). Ürümchi: Xinjiang shaonian.

Pike, John. 1999. "Uyghur Militants Committee for Eastern Turkistan." *Federation of American Scientists Intelligence Resource Program*, accessed online at www.fas.org/irp/world/para/uighur.htm, on Nov. 11, 2004.

Pan, Philip. 2002. "China Links Bin Laden to Separatists. Report Details Attacks in Mostly Muslim Region." *Washington Post* (Jan. 22): A08.

Phillipson, Robert. 1988. "Linguacism: Structures and ideologies in linguistic imperialism." In *Minority Education: From Shame to Struggle*, ed. Tove Skutnabb-Kangas and Jim Cummins. Clevedon: Multilingual Matters.

PRC Embassy. 2004. "History and Development of Xinjiang (Part 3): White Paper." Accessed online at www.china-embassy.org/eng/zt/zfbps/t36559.htm, on Nov. 11, 2004.

Radio Free Asia. 2004. "China Imposes Chinese Language on Uyghur Schools" (Mar. 16). Accessed online at www.rfa.org/english/news/social/2004/03/16/130822/, on Nov. 11, 2004.

Rudelson, Justin. 1997. *Oasis Identities: Uyghur nationalism along China's Silk Road.* New York: Columbia University.

Sautman, Barry. 1999. "Expanding access to higher education for China's national minorities Policies of Preferential Admissions." In *China's National Minority Education, Culture, Schooling, and Development*, ed. Gerard A. Postiglione. New York: Falmer Press: 173–210.

Schiffman, Harold. 1999. "South and Southeast Asia." In *Handbook of Language and Ethnicity*, ed. Joshua Fishman. Oxford & New York: Oxford University: 431–42.

Schlyter, Birgit N. 2001. "Language Policies in Present-Day Central Asia." *MOST Journal on Multicultural Studies* 3, no. 2. Accessed online at www.unesco.org/most/vl3n2sc hlyter.htm#carlson, on Nov. 11, 2004.

Schmidt-Häuer, Christian. 2001. "Afghanistan, das umstellte Land." *Die Zeit* 44.

Shapiro, Michael C., and Harold Schiffman. 1981. *Language and Society in South Asia.* Delhi: Motilal Banarsidass.

Siegle, Joseph T., Michael M. Weinstein, and Morton H. Halperin. 2004. "Why Democracies Excel." *Foreign Affairs 83*, no. 5 (Sept./Oct.).

Skutnabb-Kangas, Tove. 1997–2004. "Definitions: Language or Dialect?" Accessed online at www.terralingua.org/Definitions/DLangDialect.html, on Nov. 11, 2004.

Slovo Kyrgyzstana. 1998. Cited in Landau & Kellner-Heinkele: 187.

So, Jenny F., and Emma C. Bunker. 1995. *Traders and Raiders on China's Northern Frontier.* Washington, DC: Arthur M. Sackler Gallery, Smithsonian Institution; Seattle: University of Washington Press.

St. John, Daniel, ed. 1993. *Uighur-English Dictionary.* Ürümchi: Xinjiang renmin.

Sugawara, Jun. 2001. 中国・新疆ウイグル自治区における文字と印刷・出版文化の歴史と現状－ウイグル語の事例 を中心に－菅 原 純 (The printing of orthographies in China's Uyghur Autonomous Region, with a focus on the History and Situation of Uyghur-language Publication Culture). Accessed online at www.aa.tufs.ac.jp/~tjun/data/gicas/xjcpp.pdf, on Feb. 20, 2004.

Swanström, Niklas. 2003. "Chinese Business Interests in Central Asia: A Quest for Dominance." *Central Asia-Caucasus Analyst* (June 18). Accessed online at cacianalyst.org/view_article.php?articleid=1495, on Nov. 11, 2004.

UNESCO Ad Hoc Expert Group on Endangered Languages. 2003. *Language Vitality and Endangerment.* UNESCO. Accessed online at http://portal.unesco.org/culture/en/file_download.php/21b5446d3321dc495911144b59200105language_vitality_and_endangerment.pdf, on Nov. 19, 2004.

Von Baratta, Mario, ed. 2000. *Der Fischer Weltalmanach 2001.* Frankfurt: Fischer.

Wadley, Stephen A. 1996. "Altaic Influences on Beijing Dialect: The Manchu Case." *Journal of the American Oriental Society* 116, no. 1: 99–104.

Wali, Qurban. 1986. *Bizning Tarihiy Yeziqlirimiz* (Our Historical Orthographies). Ürümchi: Shaonian.

Wang Weidong and the Xinjiang Uygur Autonomous Region Nationalities Language and Script Committee. 1992. "Xinjiang da zhong xiao xue Hanyu jiaoxue qingkuang yu jingyan" (The conditions and experience of Chinese-language primary, secondary and tertiary education in Xinjiang). In *Zhongguo shaoshu minzu yuyan wenzi shiyong he fazhan wenti* (Issues in the Use and Development of Chinese Minority Languages and Scripts), ed. Chinese Academy of Social Sciences Nationalities Institute and National Committee on Nationality Affairs. Beijing: China Tibetan Studies Publishing: 246–51.

Wei Cuiyi. 1993. "A Historical Survey of Modern Uighur Writing since the 1950s in Xinjiang, China." *Central Asiatic Journal* 37, no. 3/4: 249–322.

Weinreich, Max. 1945. "Der yivo un di problemen fun undzer tsayt" (Yivo and the problems of our time). *Yivo-bleter* 25.1.13.

Working, Russell. 2001. "Fighting for Independence in the shadow of Goliath." *Japan Times* (Nov. 6).

Xinhua News Agency. 2003. "Comparative Version of the White Paper on History, Development of Xinjiang" (May 26).

Xinjiang Academy of Social Sciences. 1994. *Fan yisilan zhuyi, fan Tujue zhuyi yanjiu* (Research on Pan-Islamism and Pan-Turkism): 47–48. Internal circulation publication.

Xinjiang University, eds. 2003. *Han-Ying-Wei keji cidian* (A Science and Technology Dictionary of Chinese, English, and Uyghur). Ürümchi: Xinjiang University.

Xinjiang Uygur Autonomous Region Nationality Language and Script Task Committee, eds. 1985. *Hazirqi zaman Uyghur ädäbiy tilining imla lughiti* (An Orthographic Dictionary of Modern Literary Uyghur). Ürümchi: Renmin.

Xinjiang Uighur Autonomous Regional Working Committee of Minorities' Language and Writing. 2004. Accessed online at www.xjyw.gov.cn/index.htm, on August 21, 2004.

Xu Chaoren and Zhang Leijun. 1997. *Xinbian Minzuguan Minzu Zhengce Gailun* (An Introduction To Nationalities and Nationalities Policy Education, New Edition). Ürümchi: Xinjiang Renmin.

Yaqub, Abliz et al. 1990–1999. *Uyghur tilining izahliq lughiti* (An Explanatory Dictionary of the Uyghur Language), Vols. 1–6. Beijing: Minzu.

Yi Kunxiu and Gao Shijie, eds. *Jichu Weiwueryu/Uyghur tilidin asas* (Elementary Uyghur). Beijing: Central Minorities Institute, 1991.

Yom, Sean L. 2002. "Uighurs Flex their Muscles." *Asia Times Online* (Jan. 23). Accessed online at www.atimes.com/china/DA23Ad01.html, on Nov. 11, 2004.

Yunus, Khojaahmet. 1996. *Til-Tärjimä wä atalghular toghrisida* (On Language, Translation, and Terminology). Ürümchi: Xinjiang shehui kexue.

Yüsüp, Israpil et al., eds. 1987. *Qadimki Uyghur yeziqdiki Maytri Simit* (An Old Uyghur script version of the Maytri Simit). Ürümchi: Xinjiang renmin.

Zhang Hongyou, ed. 1996. *Ying-Han shuangjie jisuanji cidian* (An English-Chinese explanatory computing dictionary). Beijing: Qinghua.

Zhao Yong and Keith P. Campbell. 1995. "English in China." *World Englishes* 14, no. 3: 377–90.

Zhonggong Chabuchaer baoshe. 1946–present. *Chabuchaer bao* (Chapchal News).

Zhonghua renmin gongheguo falü huibian 1979–1984 (Collection of Laws of the People's Republic of China 1979–1984). 1985. Beijing: Renmin.

Zhonghua Renmin Gongheguo minzu quyu zizhifa / Law of the People's Republic of China on Regional Autonomy. 2001. Beijing: Minzu.

Zhou, Minglang. 2003. *Multilingualism in China: The Politics of Writing Reforms for Minority Languages 1949–2002.* Berlin & New York: Mouton de Gruyter.

Background Information

Background of the Xinjiang Conflict

The Xinjiang Uyghur Autonomous Region, as it is officially known to the Chinese (Uyghur nationalists call it "East Turkistan" or "Uyghuristan"), is a vast region in the northwestern corner of the People's Republic of China. Occupying one-sixth the total area of China, it holds only a fraction more than 1 percent of China's population, some 18 million. Xinjiang possesses rich deposits of oil, natural gas, and nonferrous metals. Chinese officials value it as a space to absorb migrants, a source of resources crucial to economic development, and a link to Central Asia. They desperately want to maintain hold of Xinjiang, fearing its loss would incite the CCP's collapse and possibly the secession of Taiwan and Tibet.

While a succession of Qing (1644–1911), Republican (1912–49), and Communist governments all laid formal claim to the territory and inhabitants of what is today Xinjiang, locals have resented and resisted each assertion of authority. Official Chinese sources claim that Xinjiang and the Uyghurs have been part of China "since ancient times," dating incorporation to the first century B.C. Yet only in the mid-eighteenth century was the whole of the region conquered militarily from the east, and then by the Manchu Qing empire. Qing rulers made the region a province only in the late nineteenth century, fearing its loss due to foreign incursions or internal rebellion. Between 1867 and 1877, for instance, Qing rulers lost control of the region when Yaqub Beg established an independent kingdom that achieved diplomatic relations with Turkey and Britain. Opposition to rule from Beijing (and for a time Nanjing) continued after the collapse of the Manchu empire and the founding of the Republic of China in 1912: Turki leaders twice established independent states of "East Turkistan"—once briefly in the southwest from 1933 to 1934 and again more successfully in the three northwestern prefectures of Xinjiang from 1944 to 1949.

Nor has the Chinese Communist Party been immune from challenges in the region. Though the party killed, imprisoned, or co-opted nearly all advocates of independence soon after taking power in 1949, Uyghur aspirations to independence did not disappear. Uyghurs within Xinjiang organized a number of opposition parties in the first postrevolutionary decade (nearly all of them quickly squelched by the party-state). Uyghur emigrés in Soviet Central Asia and Turkey continued to harbor the dream of establishing an independent Uyghur state. While the high socialist era in Xinjiang (1958–76) witnessed little secessionist violence, Chinese officials claim to have exposed several underground organizations. In 1962 tens of thousands of Uyghurs and Kazakhs rioted in the northwest city of Ghulja, and more than 60,000 fled Xinjiang for the Soviet Union. Uyghur nationalism found renewed public expression in the Reform Era (1978–), and participants in several demonstrations in the late 1980s called for independence. Peaceful demonstrations disappeared in the wake of the Tian'anmen crackdown in 1989. Since 1990 a series of violent episodes in Xinjiang has drawn international attention. The Baren Uprising in April 1990, in which several dozen Uyghurs attacked the regional government and police, was the most violent clash. Bus bombings in Urumchi in 1992 and 1997 left over ten dead and led some to label Uyghur separatists terrorists. A peaceful demonstration in Hotan in 1995, and a much larger one in Ghulja in 1997, turned violent after police attacked the demonstrators. A spate of political assassinations of regional officials and religious clerics has created a sense of uncertainty in parts of the region. Nevertheless, since 1949 there has not been a "hot conflict" in Xinjiang like those in Palestine, Chechnya, Aceh, or Mindanao. Underground Uyghur organizations in Xinjiang are all but unheard of, and there are no independent militias. Given the relative scarcity of collective violence, no international agent has explicitly called for intervention or mediation.

Uyghur Autonomous Region, China

RUSSIA

KAZAKHSTAN

MONGOLIA

Tacheng

ALTAY

TARBAGHATAY

KARAMAY

BORTALA

SHIHEZI

CHANGJI

Ghulja

URUMQI

HAMI

Almaty

ILI

Turpan

Bishkek

TURPAN

KYRGYZSTAN

Aksu

GANSU

AKSU

Kashgar

BAYANGOL

KIZILSU

KASHGAR

Baren

Yarkand

HOTAN

Hotan

QINGHAI

PAKISTAN

TIBET
AUTONOMOUS
REGION

INDIA

0   200   400
Kilometers

NEPAL

Lhasa

Cities

Prefecture boundaries

Provincial boundaries

National boundaries

The Uyghur Autonomous Region contains
several non-Uyghur majority prefectures.
These are: Kizilsu (Kirghiz autonomous
prefecture), Altay, Tarbaghatay, and Ili
(Kazakh autonomous prefectures), Bortala
and Bayangol (Mongol autonomous
prefectures), and Changji (Hui autonomous
prefecture).

*Note: Map boundaries and locations are approximate.
Geographic features and their names do not imply
official endorsement or recognition by the UN.*

UYGHUR
AUTONOMOUS
REGION
(Xinjiang)

CHINA

Project Information

The Dynamics and Management of Internal Conflicts in Asia
Project Rationale, Purpose and Outline

Project Director: Muthiah Alagappa
Principal Researchers: Edward Aspinall (Aceh)
                        Danilyn Rutherford (Papua)
                        Christopher Collier (southern Philippines)
                        Gardner Bovingdon (Xinjiang)
                        Elliot Sperling (Tibet)

Rationale

Internal conflicts have been a prominent feature of the Asian political landscape since 1945. Asia has witnessed numerous civil wars, armed insurgencies, coups d'etat, regional rebellions, and revolutions. Many have been protracted; several have far reaching domestic and international consequences. The civil war in Pakistan led to the break up of that country in 1971; separatist struggles challenge the political and territorial integrity of China, India, Indonesia, Burma, the Philippines, Thailand, and Sri Lanka; political uprisings in Thailand (1973 and 1991), the Philippines (1986), South Korea (1986), Taiwan, Bangladesh (1991), and Indonesia (1998) resulted in dramatic political change in those countries; although the political uprisings in Burma (1988) and China (1989) were suppressed, the political systems in these countries as well as in Vietnam continue to confront problems of political legitimacy that could become acute; and radical Islam poses serious challenges to stability in Pakistan, Indonesia, Malaysia, and India. In all, millions of people have been killed in the internal conflicts, and tens of millions have been displaced. And the involvement of external powers in a competitive manner (especially during the Cold War) in several of these conflicts had negative consequences for domestic and regional security.

Internal conflicts in Asia (as elsewhere) can be traced to three issues—national identity, political legitimacy (the title to rule), and distributive justice—that are often interconnected. With the bankruptcy of the socialist model and the transitions to democracy in several countries, the number of internal conflicts over the legitimacy of political system has declined in Asia. However, political legitimacy of certain governments continues to be contested from time to time and the legitimacy of the remaining communist and authoritarian systems is likely to confront challenges in due course. The project deals with internal conflicts arising from the process of constructing national identity with specific focus on conflicts rooted in the relationship of minority communities to the nation-state. Here too many Asian states have made considerable progress in constructing national communities but several states including some major ones still confront serious problems that have degenerated into violent conflict. By affecting the political and territorial integrity of the state as well as the physical, cultural, economic, and political security of individuals and groups, these conflicts have great potential to affect domestic and international stability.

Purpose

The project investigates the dynamics and management of five key internal conflicts in Asia—Aceh and Papua in Indonesia, the Moro conflict in the southern Philippines, and the conflicts pertaining to Tibet and Xinjiang in China. Specifically it investigates the following:

1. Why (on what basis), how (in what form), and when does group differentiation and political consciousness emerge?
2. What are the specific issues of contention in such conflicts? Are these of the instrumental or cognitive type? If both, what is the relationship between them? Have the issues of contention altered over time? Are the conflicts likely to undergo further redefinition?
3. When, why, and under what circumstances can such contentions lead to violent conflict? Under what circumstances have they not led to violent conflict?
4. How can the conflicts be managed, settled, and eventually resolved? What are policy choices? Do options such as national self-determination, autonomy, federalism, electoral design, and consociationalism exhaust the list of choices available to meet the aspirations of minority communities? Are there innovative ways of thinking about identity and sovereignty that can meet the aspirations of the minority communities without creating new sovereign nation-states?
5. What is the role of the regional and international communities in the protection of minority communities?
6. How and when does a policy choice become relevant?

Design

A study group has been organized for each of the five conflicts investigated in the study. With a principal researcher each, the study groups comprise practitioners and scholars from the respective Asian countries including the region or province that is the focus of the conflict, the United States, and

Australia. For composition of study groups please see the participants list.

All five study-groups met jointly for the first time in Washington, D.C. from September 29 through October 3, 2002. Over a period of four days, participants engaged in intensive discussion of a wide range of issues pertaining to the five conflicts investigated in the project. In addition to identifying key issues for research and publication, the meeting facilitated the development of cross country perspectives and interaction among scholars who had not previously worked together. Based on discussion at the meeting five research monograph length studies (one per conflict) and twenty policy papers (four per conflict) were commissioned.

Study groups met separately for the second meeting. The Aceh and Papua study group meetings were held in Bali on June 16–17, the southern Philippines study group met in Manila on June 23, and the Tibet and Xinjiang study groups were held in Honolulu on August 20–22, 2003. The third meeting of all study groups was held in Washington, D.C. from February 28 to March 2, 2004. These meetings reviewed recent developments relating to the conflicts, critically reviewed the first drafts of the policy papers prepared for the project, reviewed the book proposals by the principal researchers, and identified new topics for research.

Publications
The project will result in five research monographs (book length studies) and about twenty policy papers.

Research Monographs. To be authored by the principal researchers, these monographs present a book-length study of the key issues pertaining to each of the five conflicts. Subject to satisfactory peer review, the monographs will appear in the East-West Center Washington series *Asian Security*, and the East-West Center series *Contemporary Issues in the Asia Pacific*, both published by the Stanford University Press.

Policy Papers. The policy papers provide a detailed study of particular aspects of each conflict. Subject to satisfactory peer review, these 15,000- to 25,000-word essays will be published in the East-West Center Washington *Policy Studies* series, and be circulated widely to key personnel and institutions in the policy and intellectual communities and the media in the respective Asian countries, United States, and other relevant countries.

Public Forums

To engage the informed public and to disseminate the findings of the project to a wide audience, public forums have been organized in conjunction with study group meetings.

Two public forums were organized in Washington, D.C. in conjunction with the first study group meeting. The first forum, cosponsored by the United States-Indonesia Society, discussed the Aceh and Papua conflicts. The second forum, cosponsored by the United States Institute of Peace, the Asia Program of the Woodrow Wilson International Center, and the Sigur Center of The George Washington University, discussed the Tibet and Xinjiang conflicts.

Public forums were also organized in Jakarta and Manila in conjunction with the second study group meetings. The Jakarta public forum on Aceh and Papua, cosponsored by the Center for Strategic and International Studies in Jakarta, and the southern Philippines public forum cosponsored by the Policy Center of the Asian Institute of Management attracted key persons from government, media, think tanks, activist groups, diplomatic community, and the public.

In conjunction with the third study group meetings, also held in Washington, D.C., three public forums were offered. The first forum, cosponsored by the United States-Indonesia Society, addressed the conflicts in Aceh and Papua. The second forum, cosponsored by the Sigur Center of The George Washington University, discussed the conflicts in Tibet and Xinjiang. A third forum was held to discuss the conflict in the southern Philippines. This forum was cosponsored by the United States Institute of Peace.

Funding Support

This project is supported with a generous grant from the Carnegie Corporation of New York.

Project Director
Muthiah Alagappa
East-West Center Washington

Aceh Study Group

Edward Aspinall
University of Sydney
Principal Researcher

Saifuddin Bantasyam
Human Rights Forum, Banda Aceh

Harold Crouch
Australian National University

Ahmad Humam Hamid
Care Human Rights, Banda Aceh

Bob Hadiwinata
University of Parahyangan, Indonesia

Konrad Huber
USAID, Washington, D.C.

Sidney Jones
International Crisis Group, Jakarta

T. Mulya Lubis
Lubis, Santosa and Maulana, Jakarta

Marcus Meitzner
USAID, Jakarta

Kelli Muddell
International Center for Transitional
  Justice, New York

Michael Ross
University of California, Los Angeles

Kirsten E. Schulze
London School of Economics

Rizal Sukma
CSIS, Jakarta

Paul Van Zyl
International Center for Transitional
  Justice, New York

Agus Widjojo
Former Chief of Staff for Territorial
  Affairs, Government of Indonesia

Sastrohandoyo Wiryono
Chief Negotiator for the Government
  of Indonesia in the peace talks with
  the Free Aceh Movement

Daniel Ziv
USAID, Jakarta

Papua Study Group

Danilyn Rutherford
University of Chicago
Principal Researcher

Ikrar Nusa Bhakti
Indonesian Institute of Sciences (LIPI),
  Jakarta

Richard Chauvel
Victoria University, Melbourne

Benny Giay
The Institute for Human Rights
  Study and Advocacy, Jayapura

Barbara Harvey
Former Deputy Chief of Mission for
  the U.S. Embassy in Indonesia

Rodd McGibbon
USAID, Jakarta

Papua Study Group continued

Octavianus Mote
Yale University

Samsu Rizal Panggabean
Gadjah Mada University, Yogyakarta

John Rumbiak
ELS-HAM, Jayapura

Barnabas Suebu
Former Governor of Irian Jaya

Agus Sumule
Universitas Negeri Papua, Amban

Southern Philippines Study Group

Christopher Collier
Australian National University
Principal Researcher

Robert F. Barnes
USAID, Philippines

Noemi Bautista
USAID, Philippines

Saturnino M. Borras, Jr.
Institute of Social Studies, The Hague

Jesus Dureza
Presidential Assistant for Mindanao,
Philippines

Alma Evangelista
United Nations Development
Programme, Manila

Eric Gutierrez
WaterAid, United Kingdom

Carolina Hernandez
Institute for Strategic and
Development Studies, Manila

Abraham S. Iribani
Assistant Secretary, Department of the
Interior and Local Government
Government of the Philippines,
Manila

Mary Judd
The World Bank, Philippines

Macapado Muslim
Mindanao State University
Fatima, General Santos City

Amina Rasul-Bernardo
Asian Institute of Management,
Manila

Steven Rood
The Asia Foundation, Philippines

David Timberman
USAID, Washington, D.C.

Michael Yates
USAID, Philippines

Tibet Study Group

Elliot Sperling
Indiana University, Bloomington
Principal Researcher

Allen Carlson
Cornell University

Shulong Chu
Tsinghua University, Beijing

Yongbin Du
Chinese Center for Tibet Studies,
Beijing

Tibet Study Group continued

Marc D. Koehler
U.S. Department of State

Carole McGranahan
University of Colorado at Boulder

Warren W. Smith, Jr
Radio Free Asia

Tashi Rabgey
Harvard University

Tseten Wangchuk
Voice of America

Xinjiang Study Group

Gardner Bovingdon
Indiana University, Bloomington
Principal Researcher

Jay Dautcher
University of Pennsylvania

Arienne Dwyer
University of Kansas

Talant Mawkanuli
Indiana University, Bloomington

James Millward
Georgetown University

Susan Shirk
University of California, San Diego

Stan Toops
Miami University

Nury Turkel
American University

Nabijan Tursun
Radio Free Asia

Shengmin Yang
Central University for Nationalities,
  Beijing

Other Participants

Allen Choate
Asia Foundation, Hong Kong

Chester Crocker
Georgetown University

Stephen Del Rosso, Jr.
Carnegie Corporation of New York

Pauline Kerr
Australian National University

Federico M. Macaranas
Asian Institute of Management,
  Manila

Christopher McNally
East-West Center

Charles Morrison
East-West Center

Holly Morrow
U.S. Department of State

Hadi Soesastro
CSIS, Jakarta

Sheila Smith
East-West Center

Arun Swamy
East-West Center

Barbara Walter
University of California, San Diego

List of Reviewers 2004–05

The East-West Center Washington would like to acknowledge the following, who have offered reviews of manuscripts for *Policy Studies*.

Pamela Aall
United States Institute of Peace

Itty Abraham
Social Science Research Council, D.C.

Patricio Nunes Abinales
Kyoto University

Muthiah Alagappa
East-West Center Washington

Edward Aspinall
The University of Sydney

Robert Barnett
Columbia University

Gardner Bovingdon
Indiana University, Bloomington

Leslie Butt
University of Victoria

Craig Calhoun
New York University

Allen Carlson
Cornell University

Harold Crouch
Australian National University

Jay Dautcher
University of Pennsylvania

June Teufel Dreyer
University of Miami

Sumit Ganguly
Indiana University, Bloomington

Brigham Golden
Columbia University

Reuel Hanks
Oklahoma State University

Eva-Lotta Hedman
University of Oxford

Paul Hutchcroft
University of Wisconsin, Madison

Yuen Foong Khong
Nuffield College, Oxford University

Sidney Jones
International Crisis Group

Stephanie Lawson
University of East Anglia

David Leheny
University of Wisconsin, Madison

R. William Liddle
The Ohio State University

Kenneth G. Lieberthal
University of Michigan

Thomas McKenna
SRI Consulting

Andrew Nathan
Columbia University

Tashi Rabgey
Harvard University

Geoffrey Robinson
University of California, Los Angeles

Michael Ross
University of California, Los Angeles

Danilyn Rutherford
University of Chicago

Kirsten E. Schulze
London School of Economics

Yitzhak Shichor
The Hebrew University of Jerusalem

Sheldon Simon
Arizona State University

Timothy Sisk
University of Denver

Anthony Smith
Asia Pacific Center for Security Studies, Honolulu

Warren W. Smith
Radio Free Asia

Elliot Sperling
Indiana University, Bloomington

Arun Swamy
East-West Center

David Timberman
USAID, D.C.

Meredith Weiss
DePaul University

Geoffrey White
East-West Center

Policy Studies
Previous Publications

Policy Studies 1
The Aceh Peace Process:
Why it Failed
    Edward Aspinall, University of
       Sydney
    Harold Crouch, Australian
       National University

Policy Studies 2
The Free Aceh Movement (GAM):
Anatomy of a Separatist Organization
    Kirsten E. Schulze, London School
       of Economics

Policy Studies 3
Security Operations in Aceh:
Goals, Consequences, and Lessons
    Rizal Sukma, Centre for Strategic
       and International Studies, Jakarta

Policy Studies 4
Beijing's Tibet Policy:
Securing Sovereignty and Legitimacy
    Allen Carlson, Cornell University

Policy Studies 5
The Papua Conflict:
Jakarta's Perceptions and Policies
    Richard Chauvel, Victoria University,
       Melbourne
    Ikrar Nusa Bhakti, Indonesian Institute
       of Sciences, Jakarta

Policy Studies 6
Violent Separatism in Xinjiang:
A Critical Assessment
    James Millward, Georgetown University

Policy Studies 7
The Tibet-China Conflict:
History and Polemics

    Elliot Sperling, Indiana University,
       Bloomington

Policy Studies 8
The Moro Conflict:
Landlessness and Misdirected State
Policies
    Eric Gutierrez, WaterAid, U.K.
    Saturnino Borras, Jr., Institute of Social
       Studies, The Hague

Policy Studies 9
The HDC in Aceh:
Promises and Pitfalls of NGO
Mediation and Implementation
    Konrad Huber, Council on Foreign
       Relations

Policy Studies 10
Secessionist Challenges in Aceh
and Papua:
Is Special Autonomy the Solution?
    Rodd McGibbon, USAID, Jakarta

Policy Studies 11
Autonomy in Xinjiang:
Han Nationalist Imperatives and
Uyghur Discontent
    Gardner Bovingdon, Indiana University,
       Bloomington

Policy Studies 12
Sino-Tibetan Dialogue in the Post-
Mao Era:
Lessons and Prospects
    Tashi Rabgey, Harvard University
    Tseten Wangchuk Sharlho,
       Independent Journalist

Policy Studies 13
Plural Society in Peril:
Migration, Economic Change, and the
Papua Conflict
    Rodd McGibbon, USAID, Jakarta

Policy Studies 14
Constructing Papuan Nationalism:
History, Ethnicity, and Adaptation
    Richard Chauvel, Victoria University,
       Melbourne